2.13.80

The
Low-Cholesterol
Food Processor
Cookbook

The Low-Cholesterol Food Processor Cookbook

SUZANNE S. JONES

Illustrated by Mona Mark

Introductory Remarks by Carl G. Sontheimer

Foreword by Kevin E. Conboy, M.D.

DOUBLEDAY & COMPANY, INC., GARDEN CITY, NEW YORK
1980

Library of Congress Cataloging in Publication Data

Jones, Suzanne S   1926–
  The low-cholesterol food processor cookbook.

  Includes index.
  1. Low-cholesterol diet—Recipes.   2. Salt-free diet
—Recipes.   3. Low-fat diet—Recipes.   4. Food
processor cookery.   I. Title.
RM237.75.J66   641.5′63
ISBN: 0-385-14745-7
Library of Congress Catalog Card Number 78–22329
Copyright © 1980 by Suzanne S. Jones

For my husband, Guy

Contents

Ill-health, of body or of mind, is defeat. . . . Health alone is victory. Let all men, if they can manage it, contrive to be healthy!

Thomas Carlyle
("Sir Walter Scott,"
London and Westminster Review,
No. 12, 1838)

Introductory Remarks

It has been some years now since we convinced Sue Jones to stop managing a gourmet foods shop (and educating its customers in the fine points of cooking), and to join us at Cuisinarts, Inc.

Ours is a rather unstructured organization, and Sue has done everything from coping with customers' problems to organizing demonstrations of our product. This book testifies to her versatility. Her recipes are both tempting and out of the ordinary: she has succeeded in offering a great variety of tastes and textures, from appetizers to desserts, all within the rigid constraints of a low-cholesterol, low-sodium, low-fat regime.

I am certain that this book will bring renewed pleasures of the table to thousands whose health requires strict adherence to that diet.

Carl G. Sontheimer, President
CUISINARTS, INC.

Foreword

For too long the efforts of medicine have been heavily concentrated on the treatment of coronary artery disease *after* the development of symptoms. The concept of treating the apparently healthy individual in the hopes of forestalling the development of coronary artery disease has to be recognized. What the healthy individual does now influences what will happen in the future. This is a difficult concept to grasp, for the rewards are not immediate but long-term.

Coronary artery disease begins and progresses for decades before the consequences of either heart attack or even death occur. That there is an association between coronary artery disease and factors that accelerate the progression of this disease, there is no doubt. We do not claim that such factors as elevated blood cholesterol, high blood pressure, and cigarette smoking cause heart disease. Certain epidemiologic conditions have not been met to make such a statement. The facts already known cannot, however, be ignored. First, elevated cholesterol (lipids) is associated with an increased risk of heart attack. Second, cholesterol can be lowered by diet and/or medication in most patients. The third factor that must finally be determined is whether the lowering of cholesterol will result in a reduced incidence of heart attacks. Bearing this in mind, we need not know all the causative factors of heart disease before preventive programs can be initiated.

In dealing with the individual who has known heart disease, the continuation of a preventive program is equally important, and certainly expansion into other dietary measures may well be in order. Restriction of salt intake may well become an integral part of a patient's diet, at the physician's recommendation. When this is coupled with a cholesterol-lowering regimen, difficulties may arise. Therefore, one diet adhering closely to both lowering cholesterol and limiting salt intake becomes essential. If that dietary regimen is positive and appealing to the individual, then the negativeness of dieting will be avoided.

श्र श्र श्र 3

Meal planning must be a positive experience, allowing for a wide variation of choice, eliminating restrictions and self-denial. This will help ensure a greater compliance with the program recommended by the patient's physician and therefore contribute to a healthier life-style.

Mrs. Jones's book emphasizes a diet that *is* positive and appealing. It offers a range of recipes that should be considered not only by a person who has a heart condition but, equally important, by the individual concerned with long-term health rewards.

Her book specifically takes into account the day-to-day meal planning so essential to such a diet. With its wide variety of recipes from appetizers to desserts, all of which satisfy the requirements of a low-cholesterol, low-sodium, low-fat diet, the book is both a lifesaver and a delight.

Kevin E. Conboy, M.D.,
CARDIOLOGIST,
GREENWICH, CONNECTICUT

Author's Introduction

This is a cookbook of low-cholesterol, low-sodium, low-fat recipes adapted for the food processor.

It came about during my second year at Cuisinarts, Inc., when my husband had a mild heart attack and was restricted to a low-cholesterol, low-sodium, low-fat diet.* It was then that I rediscovered the advantages of the food processor. It saves untold time, of course; affords ease and accuracy in preparation; provides the opportunity of making dishes that would otherwise be too complicated; and extends the range of recipe selection. But in this diet, with the proper recipes and choice of ingredients, the food processor will help provide a thoroughly appealing, satisfying, and attractive low-cholesterol, low-sodium, low-fat meal.

Statistics inform us that heart disease is the greatest American killer, and that cardiovascular diseases cause more than one half of all deaths today. More than a million people a year suffer from heart attacks. Almost half that number die.

There are no statistics available on how many heart patients have access to a food processor, but the number is definitely increasing. Cuisinarts, Inc., is deluged by requests for low-cholesterol, low-sodium, low-fat recipes. We have demonstrators in some areas who give classes to coronary outpatients and their families on preparation of suitable diets using the food processor.

There are over twenty food processors on the market today with varying degrees of performance. The Cuisinart® food processor remains the standard, however, as it has been from the beginning, and all recipes in this book were tested with that machine. Should you own another food processor and encounter a problem with any of the recipes, particularly with chopping meat or making yeast dough, halve the suggested amounts.

---

* He is now fully recovered and restrictions have been relaxed. He continues, however, to follow this diet because it helps control weight and fosters general good health.

The results should be satisfactory. Always check the instruction manual accompanying your particular machine, however, since it has specific instructions on its capabilities.

At the onset of my husband's new regimen I found and researched a multitude of cookbooks available for either the low-cholesterol, the low-sodium, or the low-fat diets. One important discovery that emerged during my research was that no single cookbook really took into account the interrelationship of cholesterol, sodium, and triglycerides. I found that in many low-sodium cookbooks the use of high-cholesterol ingredients was excessive: for example, egg yolks, whole eggs, organ meats, shellfish, sour cream, and cheese. In many of the low-cholesterol cookbooks, salt and foods or condiments high in salt content such as soy sauce, Worcestershire sauce, capers, pickles, baking powder, and baking soda were freely used. The importance of triglycerides was rarely mentioned at all, and information on which foods to avoid almost never correlated with low-cholesterol or low-sodium diets or recipes. Each heart patient is an individual case and only the patient's own doctor can prescribe the proper, most effective diet.

In addition to the available cookbooks, there are dictionaries, charts, and booklets listing the cholesterol, fat, and sodium level for hundreds of foods. The American Heart Association has several pamphlets that are extremely helpful. There is a wealth of reference information available in libraries, at bookstores, and free for the asking from many companies about saturated, monounsaturated, and polyunsaturated fats, cholesterol, lipids, food composition, and calorie count.

I selected and added all promising materials to my shelves, along with a very significant aid, the YES, NO, AND SOMETIMES food list that the hospital dietician and the patient's doctor provide. Having all this information handy can make the "coronary" cook feel more secure, just as owning one of the big, all-inclusive reference cookbooks makes any cook feel secure. It can also be overwhelming, however, when all one wants is a selective group of recipes that can be prepared easily and that one knows are *safe*, recipes that taste good, look good, and make the dieter feel good on that DAY-TO-DAY-TO-DAY syndrome of menu planning.

This cookbook, then, is the result of thorough research, considerable experimentation, and my experience at Cuisinarts, Inc., in adapting recipes for the food processor. It is a cookbook not only for heart patients, but for all those seeking a low-cholesterol, low-sodium, low-fat diet who are fortunate enough to own a Cuisinart or other food processor. It is a cookbook incorporating all areas of dietary concern to the heart patient —a cookbook concentrating on main-course dishes, soups, salads, and vegetables. It is a cookbook that will convince the "coronary" cook and the patient that this diet can be a rewarding, gastronomic experience!

Information You Should Know About...

Food Processors

As I mentioned in the introduction, there are more than twenty different brands of food processors on the market at this time. Although they are all basically the same in design and come with standard shredding and slicing discs and a steel knife—for chopping, mixing, and puréeing—all processors differ in power, work bowl capacity, shape of feed tube, and method of on/off control. The operation of the machine is quite simple, but because specific operating instructions do vary, it is important that you read and follow carefully the instructions in the manual that comes with each food processor.

The recipes in this book use the basic techniques of chopping, puréeing (an extension of chopping), slicing, shredding, and mixing or blending. There should be no problems in following the specific instructions in each recipe. These recipes were all tested with the Cuisinart food processor. Should you have any difficulty, especially in chopping meat or mixing yeast dough, halve the recipe or check the instruction manual of your particular machine.

Following is some basic information that should be helpful in using a food processor with the recipes in this book.

When using the STEEL KNIFE, the on-and-off technique controls the texture of the food being processed. In some instances, it keeps the ingredients being processed from climbing the sides of the bowl, thus eliminating the need to scrape the bowl down and ensuring a more even chop. If the machine has a pulse control, use this as the on-and-off control. when using the steel knife, it is also important to cut the food into fairly even pieces—1 to 1½ inches for vegetables or fruits (about 1½ cups at a time in the processor bowl) and 1 inch for meats (about 1 cup at a time for most efficient chopping). For processing larger amounts, do several batches. The food processor is so fast that it takes only seconds to empty the work bowl, and the results will be more satisfactory.

When processing liquid ingredients, lift off the processor work bowl with the blade in position. This forms a seal, preventing leakage. Place a finger on top of the steel knife or place your index finger in the hole in the bottom, holding the steel knife in place, when pouring mixtures out of the bowl. This prevents accidental dropping of the steel knife.

When using the SLICING DISC, cut food into lengths (ends flat) to fit the feed tube and fill it snugly. When you turn the machine on, do not hesitate with the pusher. Use medium pressure with firm foods, light pressure with soft foods. If the recipe calls for fewer sliced ingredients than will fill the feed tube snugly, fit the ingredients to be sliced on the right side of the feed tube if your machine has clockwise rpm's (true of the Cuisinart food processor) and on the left side of the feed tube if the machine has counterclockwise rpm's. As you turn the machine on, use medium pressure with the feed tube. If the food still tilts and the slices aren't even, in most cases the finished dish will not suffer.

The MEDIUM SLICING DISC will also slice firmly cooked, chilled meats and raw meats that are chilled through, but not frozen, in the freezer. Again, check the instructions with each particular machine for specific recommendations.

The shredding process is similar to the slicing process. However, to get maximum length in the food being shredded with the SHREDDING DISC, cut the ingredients to fit the feed tube horizontally.

I have recommended the FRENCH FRY DISC in some recipes. This is an optional disc available for the Cuisinart food processor and some other brands. It makes attractive, slightly curved sticks out of root vegetables, for cooking, dipping, or chilling for use in salads. It will also produce a "diced" effect with raw onions and tomatoes.

The bottom of the feed tube is slightly larger than the top. This is helpful to know when you have a lemon, onion, or any other food to be processed with the slicing, shredding, french fry or other disc, that will not quite fit through the top. Turn the top over, squeeze the food gently up through the bottom, return the cover to the bowl, and process.

The PLASTIC BLADE, a standard attachment with the Cuisinart food processor and some other brands, is recommended for salad dressings, sauces, sandwich spreads, or whenever you wish to retain some texture. The steel knife can be substituted—just watch texture carefully.

A question frequently asked during a food processor demonstration, and a complaint often expressed by a customer over the phone, is why, if the machine is so efficient, there are always small pieces of the food being processed remaining on top of the discs. If the pusher were any longer or the discs mounted on higher stems, plastic would be sliced or shredded, if the machine itself did not jam. My suggestion is to eat the remaining piece or throw it out—just as you do, without thinking, when using a hand shredder or slicer. In the case of vegetables, save them in a plastic bag in the refrigerator to use in making soup.

When shopping in the produce section of your market, keep a mental image of the feed tube in mind. In buying zucchini, yellow squash, cucumbers, potatoes, carrots, or onions, particularly for slicing, it is better to select vegetables that fit the feed tube without trimming, so that neat, whole slices are obtained. In buying for the shredding disc or the french fry disc or for use with the steel knife, size is not vital.

Substitutions and Ingredients

There are many low-sodium products on the market, as noted in the American Heart Association pamphlet of low-sodium products available. They are suggested for use in many of the recipes. A frequent ingredient is beef or chicken bouillon. If stringent salt reduction is required, use the low-sodium cubes, or make your own stock. If no additional salt is used in a recipe, and if salt is allowed, I find the MBT packets or bouillon granules the most convenient to use. This is not a salt-free diet but a sodium-reduced diet. The elimination of salt is optional, and the choice is left up to the cook. This choice will depend upon the individually prescribed diet guideline given by the doctor. There are two important rules in the preparation of this diet: (1) if there is any doubt whatsoever, check with the doctor, and (2) read all labels carefully.

All recipes calling for oil or margarine as an ingredient refer to the unsaturated variety. Unsalted margarine is also available. Because of the number of oils and margarines on the market, reading the labels is important. If the *first* oil listed is specified as "liquid," and after that some partially hardened oil is listed, that is acceptable. If the oil or margarine has anything but a "liquid" listed as the first ingredient, or has coconut oil in any form, it is certain to have an unacceptable amount of saturated fat. Coconut oil is the highest of all oils in saturated fats and is the most frequently used in "imitation" products and packaged mixes because it has a long shelf life and is less costly to the manufacturer.

Olive oil and peanut oil are listed in the group of monounsaturated fats, which indicates they neither raise nor lower cholesterol levels. Using a little for flavor now and then is permissible. You are, however, adding calories without the benefit of lowering cholesterol.

Substituting acceptable fats for unacceptable fats does not reduce calories. Fats are fats, and you still have the same number of calories per gram. However, by using skim milk, low-fat cottage cheese, lean meats, and other lower-in-calorie ingredients instead of cream, sour cream, and fatty meats, you will help monitor and control the dieter's weight as long as total calorie intake is taken into consideration.

You may think that there are no substitutes for the rich, buttery taste of classic cream dishes, but cottage cheese, skim milk, buttermilk, yogurt, and other wholesome ingredients provide their own delicious flavor. The taste may not be what you have been used to, but it will be equally as good—and better for you. You will find that French toast made with egg whites tastes just as delicious as when made with whole eggs. And no one will miss the whole eggs left out of the meat loaf.

Deviled eggs without yolks? Better than the original! It may take a while not to feel guilty about throwing away all the egg yolks. Only a certain number can be good for the dog, and the neighbors are concerned about their cholesterol, too. Get into the habit of tossing them immediately into the garbage or use them in a facial mask!

There are important differences in the cottage cheeses available for just plain eating or for use in recipes as a substitute for cream cheese or sour cream. Cottage cheese of any kind is preferable to either cream cheese or sour cream in this diet. Regular creamed cottage cheese is made from skim milk, but, because of the addition of cream and salt, the fat and sodium counts are not always as low as you may require. Skim-milk cottage cheese is much lower in fat content because no cream is added, but it does contain salt—important to know if salt is important to you. The dry-curd cottage cheese, known by several different names (pot, dry, farmer's, or hoop), are a form of skim-milk cottage cheese with a larger, dryer curd and generally have neither cream nor salt added. If you want this cheese salt-free, however, read the labels carefully. Some commercial brands that are labeled as "pot cheese" do have salt added.

Ricotta cheese, the part-skim-milk variety, made from the whey of the milk, can also be used. It is similar to cottage cheese but is sweeter in taste, does contain salt, and is somewhat higher in fat content than all cottage cheeses. It is recommended in some dessert recipes.

The only problem you might encounter in substituting pot or dry-curd cottage cheese in any recipe calling for the creamed variety would be that additional liquids must be added to ensure the recipe's success. Also, the elimination of salt from the pot cheese will make some difference to the taste of the finished dish.

There are other cheeses on the market made from skim or partly skim milk, some lower in cholesterol than others. There are also some cheese substitutes, lower in cholesterol or advertised as cholesterol-free, most of which we found unpalatable. Our decision was to have the real thing (cheese) in allowable quantities infrequently rather than waste calories, cholesterol count, and money on substitutes. This meant giving up a favorite macaroni and cheese dish chock-full of Vermont cheddar and a favorite version of Lindy's famous cheesecake. We have discovered many other fine foods, however, and feel no deprivation.

When using sugar substitutes, it is more satisfying to use half substitute and half regular sugar even though calorie content will not be reduced as much. This eliminates the aftertaste of the substitute, particularly in baked products. Adding additional flavorings or spices will also help.

Invest in a good pepper grinder. Freshly ground pepper makes a noticeable difference in every recipe calling for this frequently used seasoning.

READ ALL LABELS CAREFULLY!

𝕶 𝕶 𝕶 INFORMATION YOU SHOULD KNOW ABOUT . . .

Foods in Reserve

Recipes frequently call for chopped parsley, for grated Parmesan, Romano, or sapsago cheese, or for cracker or bread crumbs. With the food processor, it is easy to keep a supply of these ingredients on hand, and it is important in this diet, especially with crumbs, to know they are low-sodium and low-fat.

Chopped parsley When the parsley looks fresh in the market, buy several bunches. Remove the stem ends (to chop separately, or to use for flavoring soups or meats). Wash and DRY thoroughly. There is no easy way to dry parsley, except to spread it out on several layers of paper towel, turn it frequently, and change the paper towels frequently. This is important. If the parsley is not dry you will end up with a purée rather than a mince. With the steel knife in place, chop the parsley sprigs in batches (about 1 to 1½ cups, firmly packed, at one time). Turn the machine on and off, then let run until desired fineness is obtained. Pack lightly and tightly closed in plastic containers or bags and freeze. Whenever a recipe calls for chopped parsley, simply remove amount called for from the freezer. This freshly chopped, frozen parsley is far better than the dry variety.

Freshly grated sapsago, Parmesan, or Romano cheese I was unfamiliar with sapsago cheese until my research for this diet. It is made from slightly sour skim milk, is light green in color, very hard, pungent, and generally flavored with powdered clover leaves. It has a very distinct flavor. Smaller quantities than Parmesan or Romano are required for flavoring. Sapsago is slightly lower in cholesterol than Parmesan or Romano and recommended for that reason. It takes a while to get used to the flavor, but this cheese adds interest to many dishes.

Parmesan and Romano, both made from skim or partly skim milk, are allowed in restricted amounts in this diet and certainly add flavor to many recipes.

To grate any of the above, with steel knife in place, cut cheese into 1-inch pieces. With machine running, drop cheese through feed tube (2½ to 3 ounces at a time) and let machine run until cheese is finely grated. Repeat until you exhaust your supply. Grate a cupful or more, as it keeps well. Store in tightly covered plastic containers in refrigerator.

Crumbs A wonderful way to use up the remains of boxes of cereal (cornflakes or shredded wheat), crackers (unsalted or with unsalted tops), French bread, salt-free bread, or your own homemade bread. All can be reduced to crumbs in the food processor, using the steel knife. They are all preferable to any commercially packaged crumbs. Cornflakes and shredded wheat are particularly recommended in this diet.

Process a good supply and keep tightly covered. You will find them put to good use in many of the recipes.

Cheese Crumbs These are a nice "reserve" to sprinkle on top of oven-going dishes, or to make otherwise plain vegetables look and taste more interesting. To ½ cup of suggested crumbs (above), add 1 teaspoon grated sapsago cheese or 1 tablespoon grated Parmesan or Romano cheese. Work in 1 tablespoon oil or margarine. Keep tightly covered in refrigerator.

Flavored butters Flavored butters are easily made in the food processor. They add interest to sandwiches and are delicious when spread on toast or bread rounds as a snack or hors d'oeuvre and for flavoring vegetables. Keep them on hand in small crocks or other covered containers in the refrigerator. Recipes follow.

Poached Chicken Suprêmes This basic recipe initially has nothing to do with the food processor, but the end result is a delicious base for many other recipes in the book, and a definite must "in reserve." (See index.)

WATERCRESS BUTTER

½ cup watercress leaves
½ cup margarine, cut into
  1-inch pieces

1 tablespoon lemon juice
Freshly ground black pepper

With steel knife in place, chop watercress, turning machine on and off until well minced. Add remaining ingredients and process until smooth. Refrigerate.

This is delicious on thinly sliced bread, topped with thin slices of cucumbers and/or tomatoes that have been marinated in vinegar and oil. Or, for a delicious cocktail treat, slice small onions thin, soak in ice water for an hour, dry thoroughly, and place on Melba rounds that have been spread with Watercress Butter. Sprinkle with freshly ground pepper or paprika.

Recipe can easily be doubled.

MAKES ⅔ CUP

CARAWAY SEED BUTTER

½ cup caraway seeds
½ cup margarine, cut into 1-inch pieces

With steel knife in place, add ingredients and turn machine on and off until thoroughly mixed, scraping down bowl if necessary. Refrigerate.

Delicious on rye bread or toast.

MAKES ABOUT ⅔ CUP

PARMESAN BUTTER

⅓ cup firmly packed parsley
leaves
1 tablespoon grated Parmesan
cheese (about ½ ounce)

½ cup margarine, cut into
1-inch pieces

With steel knife in place, add parsley. Turn machine on and off until finely minced. Set aside.

Add Parmesan cheese. Turn machine on and off, then let run until finely grated. Add margarine and reserved parsley. Turn machine on and off until thoroughly mixed. Refrigerate.

Recipe can be doubled.

MAKES ABOUT ⅔ CUP

CURRY BUTTER

---

2 scallions, white part only
½ cup margarine, cut into
  1-inch pieces

1 teaspoon curry powder, or to
  taste

With steel knife in place and with machine running, drop scallions through feed tube, turning machine on and off until finely minced. Add margarine and curry powder. Turn machine on and off until well blended.

Recipe can be doubled. Delicious on chicken, turkey, or tuna fish sandwiches. Keep refrigerated.

MAKES ½ CUP

HERB-WINE BUTTER

½ cup margarine, cut into
  1-inch pieces
¼ cup dry white wine
2 tablespoons fresh herbs
  (thyme, tarragon)

½ teaspoon dried herbs
  (oregano, Italian) or herb of
  your choice

With steel knife in place, add all ingredients, turning machine on and off until thoroughly mixed, scraping down bowl if necessary. Refrigerate.

Delicious with fish or chicken.

MAKES JUST OVER ½ CUP

SAVORY LEMON BUTTER

4 or 5 sprigs parsley
   (1 tablespoon chopped)
1 teaspoon grated lemon rind
   (2 strips lemon zest)
½ teaspoon sugar (or
   substitute)
½ cup margarine, cut into
   1-inch pieces

1 tablespoon lemon juice
Salt (if allowed) or salt
   substitute, or omit
Pinch of savory and/or
   rosemary

With steel knife in place, chop parsley, turning machine on and off. Set aside. Add lemon zest and sugar to work bowl. Turn machine on and off, then let run until rind is finely minced. Add remaining ingredients and reserved parsley. Turn machine on and off, scraping down bowl if necessary. Refrigerate.

Recipe can be doubled. Delicious on steak, chopped meats, fish, or chicken.

MAKES JUST OVER ½ CUP

MUSHROOM BUTTER

See index.

PEANUT BUTTER

No food processor cookbook should be published without including one of the most popular functions of the food processor—making peanut butter. I have read that peanut butter is the number one sandwich choice of children from two to seventeen years of age. Judging from the enthusiastic reception of this food processor—made peanut butter at demonstrations, I think you could increase that age span from two to ninety-seven. There are none of the additives included in the commercial brands. Even the low-sodium peanut butter on the market has hydrogenated oil in the list of ingredients, which, to cholesterol-conscious cooks, means it is high in saturated fat.

Dry roasted peanuts—in 2-cup batches or less
Oil, if necessary—with dry-roasted nuts, you may find the butter
   too stiff for easy spreading

You can process up to 2 cups of peanuts at a time in the Cuisinart food processor. Check the suggested capacity of your particular food processor. With steel knife in place, turn the machine on and off, then, as the nuts become coarsely chopped, let the machine run until paste forms. You may have to scrape down the sides.

If you find the nut butter too stiff, add a few drops of oil at a time with the machine running.

Try a slice of chilled pineapple, placed on crisp greens, with a teaspoon (or more) of freshly made peanut butter in the center of the pineapple. A simple and delicious salad.

Or combine equal amounts of peanut butter and margarine in processor and chill until firm. Use as a canapé spread or open-face sandwich spread, topped with thinly sliced apples.

POACHED CHICKEN SUPRÊMES

Although this recipe does not make use of the food processor directly, the end result is the main ingredient in many other delicious recipes in this cookbook.

This is an expandable recipe that basically calls for:

*4 to 6 whole, boned and
    skinned chicken breasts, split
¾ cup chicken bouillon
    (low-sodium, if desired)*

*½ cup dry white wine
Freshly ground black pepper*

Preheat oven to 400° F.

Prepare chicken breasts by tucking ends under and placing side by side in baking dish just large enough to hold, snugly, however many you are poaching.

Combine bouillon and wine and pour over chicken breasts. Insert fork or knife between all the breasts to make certain liquid reaches between them. Sprinkle with freshly ground pepper. Cover tightly with double thickness of aluminum foil. Bake for 35 minutes.

These are delicious just as they come from the oven—tender and juicy. Or you now have a reserve to use in salads, sandwiches, hors d'oeuvre, chicken loaf, or . . .

SERVES 6

Hors d'Oeuvre

About Hors d'Oeuvre

Alcohol affects blood triglycerides as well as adding calories. For those reasons, the cocktail hour has almost become extinct for many people on a low-cholesterol, low-sodium, low-fat diet.

The following recipes for hors d'oeuvre have a definite place in the book, however. When entertaining, it is important to have tasty, allowable food available for both dieter and guest that does not advertise itself as diet food. Calories should be watched. "Low-cholesterol" does not necessarily mean "low-calorie."

The food processor facilitates the preparation of these recipes. The slicing and french fry discs turn vegetables into crisp slices and curved sticks to substitute for crackers or breads in some instances.

These are hors d'oeuvre to keep the cocktail hour healthy.

CHEESE-CURRY DIP FOR VEGETABLES

½ cup watercress leaves
3 scallions, white part only
1 (8-ounce) container low-fat
  creamed cottage cheese
1 tablespoon catsup
  (low-sodium, if desired)

Curry powder to taste
Salt (if allowed) or salt
  substitute, or omit
Crisp raw vegetables

With steel knife in place, chop watercress, turning machine on and off until well minced. With machine running, add scallions through feed tube and, turning machine on and off, mince with watercress. Add cottage cheese. Turn machine on and off, then let machine run until mixture is smooth. Add catsup and season to taste. Turn machine on and off to mix.

Serve with crisp raw vegetables: carrot slices, celery sticks, cucumber slices or sticks, cauliflower flowerets, zucchini slices or sticks.

The vegetables can be sliced with the slicing disc, and the curved sticks can be obtained by using the french fry disc. Chill vegetables in ice water to obtain optimum crispness.

MAKES 1½ CUPS

CARROT NIBBLERS

1 pound carrots, peeled
1¼ cups white wine vinegar
¼ cup sugar (or substitute)
1 teaspoon celery seed

1 teaspoon mustard seed
Salt (if allowed) or salt
    substitute to taste, or omit

Cut carrots in lengths to fit crosswise in feed tube. With french fry disc in place, process all the carrots, emptying bowl as it fills.

Heat remaining ingredients in large saucepan, add carrots, bring to a boil, and simmer, covered, until just tender (about 6 to 8 minutes). Let carrots cool in liquid and chill thoroughly overnight. Drain and serve as a cocktail nibble or as a side-dish relish.

SERVES 8 TO 10 AS A COCKTAIL NIBBLE
SERVES 4 TO 6 AS A RELISH

STUFFED CUCUMBER CANAPÉS

3 medium to large cucumbers
1 (7¾-ounce) can salmon,
    drained

3 to 4 tablespoons mayonnaise
    (see index), or enough to
    moisten

1 tablespoon lemon juice   ½ teaspoon dried dill weed
Paprika   Melba toast rounds (optional)
1 teaspoon chopped fresh dill or   Salad greens (optional)

Cut ends off cucumbers and remove seeds. Peel cucumbers and soak in lightly salted ice water for 15 minutes. Drain thoroughly and dry.

With plastic (or steel) knife in place, mix salmon and remaining ingredients, turning machine on and off just enough to mix well.

Pack cucumbers solidly with mixture. Wrap tightly and chill thoroughly for several hours.

Cut in ½-inch slices. Serve plain or on Melba toast rounds. Served on salad greens, these make a delicious luncheon salad.

Variation: Substitute tuna for salmon.

MAKES ABOUT 36 SLICES
SERVES 12 AS AN HORS D'OEUVRE
SERVES 8 TO 10 AS A SALAD

STUFFED EGGS

This is the way to offer "deviled" eggs to the dieter—you throw away ALL the egg yolks.

You will need at least 1 egg (or 2 stuffed halves) per person. Hard-boil the eggs. When cool enough to handle, peel, cut in half, and THROW AWAY THE EGG YOLKS.

The stuffing can be your choice. Any meat or fish salad is excellent; try leftover, chopped vegetables bound with a little mayonnaise and mustard, or:

½ cup cooked lamb or beef
3 scallions, with some green
   parts
½ cup low-fat creamed cottage
   cheese

1 tablespoon catsup
   (low-sodium, if desired)
Freshly ground black pepper
Additional herbs—try mint with
   lamb, thyme with beef

With steel knife in place, chop meat fine, turning machine on and off. Be careful it does not turn into a purée. Set aside.

With machine running, drop scallions through feed tube and mince fine. Add cottage cheese and let machine run until mixture is smooth. Add reserved chopped meat and the catsup and season to taste. Turn machine on and off to mix.

This makes enough to stuff 6 eggs (12 halves). Garnish your stuffed eggs with sprigs of dill, parsley, pimiento strips.

SERVES 6

TOASTED MUSHROOM ROLL-UPS

3 scallions, white part only
½ pound fresh mushrooms
3 tablespoons margarine
1 tablespoon lemon juice
Freshly ground black pepper to
   taste
1 teaspoon any 1 of the
   following: basil, chili
   powder, rosemary, marjoram,
   thyme . . .

10 slices very thin white or
   whole wheat bread (about)
Margarine
Melted margarine

With steel knife in place and with machine running, drop scallions through feed tube. Add mushrooms to bowl and mince with scallions. Melt the 3 tablespoons margarine in heavy skillet and sauté mushrooms and scallions over medium heat for 6 minutes, stirring constantly. Add lemon juice and seasonings and chill thoroughly.

Remove crusts from bread. Roll slices as flat as possible with rolling pin. Spread lightly with margarine. Using about 1 teaspoon of the mushroom filling per slice, spread evenly to edges of bread. Roll up tightly, place seam side down on lightly oiled cookie sheet, and brush with the melted margarine. Roll-ups can be frozen at this point.

To serve: preheat oven to 400° F. Remove rolls from freezer. Cut crosswise into 2 or 3 pieces. Bake on lightly oiled cookie sheet for 10 to 15 minutes, or until lightly browned.

MAKES ABOUT 24 TO 30 ROLL-UPS

SWEDISH-STYLE MEATBALLS

2 cups cornflakes (about)
1 pound very lean round steak, cut into 1-inch cubes
½ pound very lean veal, cut into 1-inch cubes
1 tablespoon dried minced onion
½ cup skim milk
1 tablespoon oil

½ teaspoon nutmeg
¼ teaspoon ground coriander
½ teaspoon grated lemon rind (I use prepared in this recipe)
Freshly ground black pepper to taste
Simmering and Serving Sauce (recipe follows)

Preheat oven to 400° F.

With steel knife, whirl enough cornflakes to make 1 cup crumbs. Place in large mixing bowl.

Trim meat well. Using about 1 cup of 1-inch cubes at a time, chop meat in batches, turning machine on and off until desired consistency is obtained. Add to crumbs in bowl. Add remaining ingredients (except sauce) and mix thoroughly with hands. Shape into bite-size balls and place on oiled cookie sheets. This can be done ahead.

Bake meatballs about 15 minutes. Remove immediately from cookie sheets.

SIMMERING AND SERVING SAUCE

1 (1-pound) can whole-berry
   cranberry sauce
2 cups beef bouillon
   (low-sodium, if desired)

1½ tablespoons cornstarch
2 tablespoons cold water

In large skillet with lid, or large top-of-stove casserole, dissolve cranberry sauce over low heat, stirring constantly. Add beef bouillon and bring to a simmer. Mix cornstarch with water and add to cranberry-bouillon mixture, stirring until slightly thickened. Add meatballs and simmer gently, covered, for about 30 minutes. Serve in chafing dish.

MAKES 50 OR MORE MEATBALLS AS AN HORS D'OEUVRE
MEATBALLS CAN BE MADE LARGER AND USED FOR A MAIN
COURSE: SERVES 6 TO 8

CURRIED SHRIMP ROLL-UPS

¼ cup parsley sprigs
3 scallions, white part only
¾ cup margarine
1½ teaspoons curry powder
 (or to taste)
3 tablespoons mayonnaise (see
 index)

6 ounces cooked shrimp (if
 using frozen, defrost, drain
 well, and dry thoroughly)
16 slices very thin white or
 whole wheat bread (about)
Melted margarine

With steel knife in place, mince parsley and set aside.

With machine running, drop scallions through feed tube and mince well. Add margarine, curry powder, and mayonnaise. Turn on and off until thoroughly creamed. Add shrimp and turn on and off until shrimp are well minced. Add reserved parsley and turn machine on and off just to mix.

Cut crusts from bread. With rolling pin, roll slices as flat as possible. Using 1 heaping teaspoon of shrimp mixture per slice, spread evenly to edges of bread. Roll up tightly. Brush with melted margarine and place seam side down on lightly oiled cookie sheet. Roll-ups can be frozen at this point.

To serve: preheat oven to 400° F. Remove roll-ups from freezer. Cut crosswise into 3 pieces. Bake on cookie sheet for 10 to 15 minutes or until browned.

MAKES ABOUT 48 ROLL-UPS

SPINACH AND SAPSAGO DIP

1 (10-ounce) package frozen
   chopped spinach
1 teaspoon chopped sapsago
   cheese
½ cup pot cheese
½ cup plain low-fat yogurt
2 tablespoons mayonnaise (see
   index)
1 tablespoon lemon juice

2 tablespoons grated fresh onion
   or 1 teaspoon dried minced
   onion flakes
Salt (if allowed) or salt
   substitute, or omit
Freshly ground black pepper
Buttermilk (optional)
Raw vegetables

Cook spinach only long enough to separate. Drain thoroughly (this is important).

With steel knife in place, chop sapsago cheese finely. Add pot cheese and process until completely smooth. Add yogurt, mayonnaise, lemon juice, onion, and salt (if used) and pepper to taste and turn on and off until blended. Add spinach and turn on and off to chop and incorporate. Check seasoning and thin with buttermilk, if necessary, to attain dip consistency.

Serve with crisp raw vegetables: carrot slices, celery sticks, cucumber sticks or slices, cauliflower flowerets, broccoli flowerets, zucchini sticks or slices, turnip sticks.

The vegetables can be sliced with the slicing disc and curved sticks can be obtained by using the french fry disc. Chill vegetables in ice water to obtain optimum crispness.

MAKES ABOUT 2 CUPS DIP

WATER CHESTNUT-CREAM CHEESE CANAPÉS

2 to 3 cucumbers or zucchini
1 (8-ounce) package Kraft
  Imitation Cream Cheese
1½ teaspoons Worcestershire
  sauce (low-sodium, if
  desired)

1 (8-ounce) can water
  chestnuts, well drained
Parsley sprigs, watercress, or
  thinly sliced pickled beets for
  garnish

Wash but do not peel cucumbers or zucchini, and cut ends flat. With slicing disc in place, cut cucumbers or zucchini in lengths to fit upright in feed tube. If too large to fit into top, insert from bottom of feed tube. Slice and set aside, making certain slices are well drained and dry.

With steel knife in place, process imitation cream cheese and Worcestershire sauce, turning machine on and off several times. Add water chestnuts and continue turning on and off, scraping down sides when necessary, until water chestnuts are well chopped but still retain a coarse texture.

Spread mixture on cucumber or zucchini slices and garnish with parsley, watercress, or thinly sliced pickled beets. Refrigerate until serving time.

MAKES 48 OR MORE CANAPÉS

SESAME CHEESE SQUARES

½ cup toasted sesame seeds
1 tablespoon grated sapsago or 2
 tablespoons grated Parmesan
 cheese
2 cups unsifted all-purpose flour
1 teaspoon baking powder (1½
 teaspoons low-sodium)

Salt (if allowed) or salt
 substitute, or omit
¼ cup margarine, cut into
 1-inch pieces
¼ cup oil
¼ cup skim milk

To toast sesame seeds, preheat oven to 350° F. Spread seeds in pie pan and brown in oven. Cool thoroughly.

With steel knife in place, grate sapsago or Parmesan cheese. Add flour, baking powder, and salt, if used, to taste. Turn machine on and off to mix thoroughly. Add margarine and turn machine on and off until mixture resembles coarse meal. Add sesame seeds, turn machine on and off. Combine oil and milk and pour into work bowl. Turn machine on and off until dough forms. Chill for at least 2 hours.

Preheat oven to 400° F.

Roll out chilled dough on lightly floured surface to about ⅛ inch. With pastry wheel or sharp knife, cut into 1- to 1½-inch squares. Arrange 1 inch apart on lightly oiled baking sheets and bake about 15 minutes.

MAKES SEVERAL DOZEN

CHICKEN-ALMOND CANAPÉS

MUSHROOM BUTTER

3 ounces fresh mushrooms (½ cup chopped)

½ cup margarine, cut into 1-inch pieces

Salt (if allowed) or salt substitute, or omit

Freshly ground pepper

CHICKEN-ALMOND SPREAD

½ cup toasted unsalted almonds

1 large stalk celery, cut into 1-inch pieces

1½ cups boneless cooked chicken (½ pound), cut into 1-inch cubes

3 to 4 tablespoons mayonnaise (see index), or enough to bind mixture well

Salt (if allowed) or salt substitute, or omit

Thinly sliced bread rounds, toasted on one side

Sliced pitted black olives or sliced truffles for garnish

To make Mushroom Butter, with steel knife in place, mince mushrooms, turning machine on and off. Add margarine and salt (if used) and freshly ground pepper to taste. Turn machine on and off until well blended. Set aside.

To make Chicken-Almond Spread, with steel knife in place, chop almonds and set aside. Chop celery, using on and off turns until coarsely chopped. Add chicken, turning machine on and off until coarsely chopped. Add mayonnaise and salt (if used) to taste and turn on and off to mix. Add reserved almonds and again turn on and off until evenly distributed.

Spread bread rounds, toasted on one side, with the Mushroom Butter—on the untoasted side. Spread the chicken-almond mixture over the top and garnish with slices of pitted black olives or truffles.

MAKES ABOUT 48 CANAPÉS

LOW-CAL STUFFED CELERY

1 (12-ounce) container pot cheese	3 celery hearts, cut into 1½-inch pieces
3 ounces Roquefort or bleu cheese, crumbled	Minced parsley or pimiento strips for garnish (optional)

With steel knife in place, whirl the pot cheese until it is completely smooth. Add the Roquefort or bleu cheese, crumbled, and continue running machine, scraping down sides as necessary, until completely blended. With machine running, add a few drops of water. This fluffs the mixture. Refrigerate.

Wash, dry, and cut celery into 1½-inch lengths. Fill with cheese mixture. Garnish with minced parsley or pimiento strips, if desired.

Variation: Add 2 or 3 minced scallions, white part only, to cheese mixture.

MAKES 36 TO 48 CELERY PIECES

QUICK SALMON MOUSSE

1 cup evaporated skim milk,
  well chilled
1 (1-pound) can red salmon
1 envelope (1 tablespoon)
  unflavored gelatin
2 tablespoons lemon juice
1 small onion, peeled and
  quartered
½ cup boiling water

½ teaspoon dry mustard
½ cup mayonnaise (see index)
¼ teaspoon sweet paprika
1 tablespoon snipped fresh dill
  or 1 teaspoon dried dill weed
Mayonnaise (optional)
Cucumber Sauce I (recipe
  follows; optional)
Melba rounds or toast triangles

Place milk in freezer so it will be very cold. If a few ice crystals form, so much the better.

Drain salmon well, discarding bones and skin, and set aside.

With steel knife in place, empty the gelatin into work bowl. Add the lemon juice, onion, boiling water, and mustard. Blend, turning on and off, until onion is completely liquefied. Add the ½ cup mayonnaise, the reserved salmon, and the paprika and dill and blend until smooth. Pour in chilled milk and let machine run for 20 seconds.

Lightly oil a 4-cup mold. Pour salmon mixture into mold and refrigerate until firm, at least 3 to 4 hours. Unmold and serve with mayonnaise or Cucumber Sauce I.

C880215

CUCUMBER SAUCE I

1 large cucumber, peeled
1 cup mayonnaise (see index)
½ teaspoon prepared mustard
  (low-sodium, if desired)

1 tablespoon lemon juice
1 tablespoon snipped fresh dill
  or 1 teaspoon dried dill weed

With shredding disc in place, shred cucumber. Remove and drain well, pressing out as much liquid as possible. With steel knife in place, return cucumber to work bowl and add remaining ingredients. Turn machine on and off just to blend.

Serve with Melba rounds or toast triangles. Also delicious for a luncheon or buffet dinner.

SERVES 25 TO 30 AS AN APPETIZER
SERVES 4 TO 6 AS A LUNCHEON COURSE

CRISPY OVEN FRIES

See index for this recipe, which makes a crispy, tasty cocktail nibble. Try sprinkling with seasoned salt (low-sodium, if desired) for an interesting flavor.

Soups

About Soup

Making soup in the food processor is so fast, simple, and flexible, I am reminded of the Mock Turtle's song from *Alice in Wonderland* by Lewis Carroll:

> Beautiful Soup, so rich and green,
> Waiting in a hot tureen!
> Who for such dainties would not stoop?
> Soup of the evening, beautiful Soup!

The food processor brings out the flavor of ingredients, aerating them to a consistency that cannot be achieved otherwise.

Leftover cooked vegetables of almost any variety, whirled to a purée in the food processor, transferred to a saucepan with an equal amount of liquid—beef or chicken bouillon, the liquid in which the vegetables were cooked (to utilize all vitamins), skim milk, or evaporated skim milk—seasoned to taste with freshly ground pepper, herbs, spices, or wine, and heated just to boiling, stirring frequently, produce that beautiful soup.

Since the food processor is more efficient at puréeing thick mixtures than thin ones, to obtain the smoothest soup process the cooked vegetables or fruits before combining them with the liquid. In some of the following recipes, however, I recommend puréeing the vegetables or fruits with the cooking liquid. It eliminates the need to drain after cooking, aerates the ingredients more thoroughly, and, in the case of starchy vegetables, eliminates the possibility of overprocessing to a sticky paste.

In most cases, there is no need for any additional thickening ingredients, particularly if potatoes are part of the purée. If the soup is too thin, however, purée more vegetables or cooked potatoes and add. If the soup is too thick, add more liquid.

The use of skim milk, mixed with dry skim milk, or evaporated skim milk gives cream soups a flavor and substance just as satisfying as those supplied by light cream.

SOUP DU JOUR
(or yesterday's vegetables regenerated)

Saturday noon we have a leisurely lunch, and it is always Soup du Jour day. That means there are two or more congenial leftover vegetables, about ½ cup each with some cooking liquid, in the refrigerator. If my husband remembers what vegetables we had recently for dinner, he will guess what today's soup may be. Otherwise he just enjoys it and asks what the special soup contains.

For example, last Saturday it was:

¼ cup peas, drained, reserving liquid

½ cup string beans, drained, reserving liquid

½ cup cauliflower, drained—cauliflower should not be saved more than overnight and the cooking liquid tends to be strong, so discard it

1 cup chicken bouillon (low-sodium, if desired)

¼ teaspoon dried thyme, rubbed in the palm of your hand before adding

⅛ teaspoon garlic powder

Freshly ground black pepper to taste

½ cup skim milk mixed with ¼ cup dry skim milk, or ½ cup evaporated milk

With steel knife in place, add vegetables to food processor. Turn machine on and off, then let run until purée is completely smooth. In heavy saucepan, add reserved liquid from vegetables, chicken bouillon, and seasonings. Stir in puréed vegetables and heat slowly to a simmer. Add milk, reheat to a simmer but do not boil, and serve.

SERVES 2 OR 3

SIMPLE SOUP DU JOUR
(without yesterday's vegetables)

It does happen, now and then, that there are no leftover vegetables for Saturday noon soup. However, if you have some raw carrots and potatoes, a simple and delicious Soup du Jour might be:

1 carrot, peeled
1 medium-size potato, peeled
2 teaspoons dried minced onion
1 cup chicken bouillon
    (low-sodium, if desired)
1 tablespoon minced parsley
    (from the freezer or dried)

¼ cup evaporated skim milk
Freshly ground black pepper
Chopped parsley or chives for
    garnish (optional)

With slicing disc in place, slice carrot and potato. Add to heavy saucepan with minced onion, bouillon, and parsley. Bring to a boil and simmer 10 to 15 minutes, or until vegetables are tender.

With steel knife in place, return vegetable mixture to work bowl and purée to smooth consistency. If you are making more than the above quantity, purée the mixture in batches.

Return to saucepan, add milk and pepper to taste, and heat to a simmer but do not boil.

This is also delicious served cold garnished with chopped parsley or chives.

SERVES 2

CORN CHOWDER

1 small onion, peeled
2 tablespoons margarine
2 small potatoes, peeled
1 (10-ounce) package frozen
  corn
2 cups chicken bouillon
  (low-sodium, if desired)

1½ cups skim milk mixed with
  ½ cup dry skim milk (plus
  more, if needed)
Salt (if allowed) or salt
  substitute, or omit
Freshly ground black pepper
Chopped parsley, dill, or chives

With slicing disc in place, slice onion. In heavy saucepan, melt margarine and sauté onion over medium heat about 10 minutes.

With slicing disc still in place, slice potatoes and add to onion. Add corn and chicken bouillon. Bring to a boil, cover, and simmer 12 to 15 minutes.

With steel knife in place, purée the vegetables with their cooking liquid in batches, returning mixture to saucepan. Add milk and salt (if used) and pepper to taste and bring slowly to a simmer but do not boil. If too thick, add more milk, but this soup should be fairly substantial.

Serve sprinkled with chopped parsley, dill, or chives.

Seasoning variations: Try ground coriander, just a pinch or so, for an interesting flavor. Try a little crumbled leaf sage—delicious.

SERVES 4

CAULIFLOWER SOUP

1 small head cauliflower,
  broken into flowerets
3 cups chicken bouillon
1 small onion, peeled and
  quartered
1 stalk celery, cut into 1-inch
  lengths
3 tablespoons margarine
2 tablespoons flour

1 cup skim milk mixed with ½
  cup dry skim milk, or 1 cup
  evaporated skim milk
Salt (if allowed) or salt
  substitute, or omit
White pepper
1 or 2 tablespoons dry sherry or
  Madeira wine, or to taste
Paprika or nutmeg

Cook cauliflower flowerets in 1 cup of the chicken bouillon until just tender. Reserve a few flowerets for decoration. With steel knife in place, purée the remaining cauliflower and cooking liquid. Set aside.

With steel knife in place, chop onion and celery, turning machine on and off until fairly fine. Melt margarine in heavy saucepan and sauté the mixture over medium heat, stirring occasionally, until tender but not browned. Add flour, stirring to mix well. Add the 2 remaining cups of bouillon slowly, stirring with a wire whisk until smooth.

Add puréed cauliflower, milk and salt (if used) and pepper to taste and heat to a simmer but do not boil. Just before serving, stir in the wine. Decorate each serving with a sprinkling of paprika (or nutmeg) and one or two of the reserved flowerets.

SERVES 6

RICE PURÉE

1 small onion, peeled and
quartered
2 tablespoons margarine
1 medium-size or 2 small
carrots, peeled
2 tablespoons uncooked rice
(not instant)
3 cups chicken bouillon
(low-sodium, if desired)

1 cup skim milk mixed with ½
cup dry skim milk, or 1 cup
evaporated skim milk
Salt (if allowed) or salt
substitute, or omit
White pepper
Chopped parsley or chives or
grated nutmeg

With steel knife in place, chop onion coarsely, turning machine on and off. Melt margarine in heavy saucepan and sauté onion over medium heat, stirring occasionally, until golden.

Cut carrots into 1-inch pieces and with steel knife, chop coarsely, using on and off turns.

Add carrots, rice, and chicken bouillon to onion. Bring to a boil and simmer, covered, for 30 minutes, or until rice is very soft.

With steel knife in place, purée the mixture in batches and return to saucepan. Add milk and season with salt (if used) and pepper to taste. Serve warm or chilled, sprinkled with chopped parsley or chives or grated nutmeg.

Variation: Add ¼ teaspoon curry powder (or to taste) to the purée and sprinkle with chopped parsley or chives.

SERVES 4 TO 6

PURÉE CRÉCY

A la Crécy is the name given to various preparations, most notably soups. Some are composed exclusively of carrots, but all include an obligatory carrot garnish. With the food processor, the preparation of this puréed soup is done with ease and speed—including the finely chopped carrots for the garnish.

1 medium-size onion, peeled
3 tablespoons margarine
5 carrots, peeled
2 potatoes, peeled
3 cups beef or chicken bouillon
  (low-sodium, if desired)

Salt (if allowed) or salt
  substitute, or omit
Freshly ground black pepper
1 or 2 tablespoons dry sherry,
  or to taste

With slicing disc in place, cut onion to fit feed tube and slice, using medium pressure.

In heavy saucepan, large enough to simmer the soup, melt margarine and sauté onion over medium heat for 5 minutes, stirring constantly.

With slicing disc still in place, slice carrots and potatoes. Reserve 5 or 6 slices of carrots and add the remaining carrots and potatoes to saucepan. Add bouillon, bring to a boil, and simmer, covered, until tender—about 10 to 12 minutes.

While soup is simmering, wipe out work bowl with paper towels. With steel knife in place, add the reserved carrot slices and mince, turning machine on and off. Remove, wrap in plastic wrap, and reserve in refrigerator.

When vegetables are tender, remove with slotted spoon. With steel knife in place, add vegetables to work bowl (1½ to 2 cups at a time) and purée, turning machine on and off, then letting it run until mixture is smooth.

Return purée to cooking liquid in saucepan and stir in well. Add salt (if used) and pepper to taste. If mixture is too thick, add some more water.

Serve sprinkled with reserved minced carrots. Try adding some sherry just before serving.

SERVES 4 TO 6

POTAGE ST. GERMAIN

This delicious pea soup is made effortlessly with the food processor.

4 to 5 scallions, white part only
1 small carrot, peeled
2 large leaves of lettuce
   (iceberg or romaine)
1 tablespoon oil or margarine
2 cups fresh or frozen peas
Pinch of sugar (or substitute)
2 cups chicken bouillon
   (low-sodium, if desired)

¾ cup skim milk mixed with
   ½ cup dry skim milk, or ¾
   cup evaporated skim milk
Dash of mace or nutmeg
   (optional)
Salt (if allowed) or salt
   substitute, or omit
Chopped parsley or chives for
   garnish

With steel knife in place and with machine running, drop scallions through feed tube. Turn machine on and off to chop. Replace steel knife with shredding disc. Shred carrot and lettuce.

In heavy saucepan, heat oil or margarine and add contents of work bowl. Sauté mixture over medium heat, stirring occasionally, for 5 minutes. Add peas, sugar, and chicken bouillon, bring to a boil, and simmer, covered, for 30 minutes.

With steel knife in place, purée mixture in batches, returning to saucepan to keep warm. Stir in milk and season to taste.

Serve hot, topped with chopped parsley or chives.

SERVES 4

MUSHROOM SOUP

If you have mushroom stems left from a recipe using only the caps, this is a delicious way to utilize them.

½ pound mushrooms (or equivalent in stems)
1 tablespoon chopped onion (½ small onion) or 1 medium-size scallion, with 1 inch green part
1 tablespoon margarine
1 tablespoon flour
1 cup chicken bouillon (low-sodium, if desired)

½ cup skim milk
Salt (if allowed) or salt substitute, or omit
1 to 2 tablespoons dry sherry, or to taste
Chopped parsley, yogurt, or lemon slices for garnish

With steel knife in place, coarsely chop the mushrooms and onion. In heavy saucepan, melt margarine and sauté the mushroom-onion mixture over medium heat, stirring occasionally, for 5 minutes. Return mixture to food processor bowl, add flour, and turn machine on and off until mixture is smooth.

Return to saucepan with chicken bouillon and milk. Add salt (if used) to taste. Heat slowly, stirring constantly—do not allow to boil. Just before serving, add sherry to taste.

Serve topped with chopped parsley, a dollop of yogurt, or a thin slice of lemon.

SERVES 2 TO 3

MAIN-DISH SOUP

Start this soup the day before you plan to serve it so that all fat can be removed from the beef broth.

1 large, meaty beef-shank bone for soup
1 tablespoon salt (if allowed) or salt substitute, or omit

The day before serving, remove meat from bone, trim, and cut into 1-inch cubes. In large heavy saucepot, cover bone and meat with water, add salt if desired, and bring to a boil. Reduce heat, cover, and simmer slowly for 3 hours, skimming occasionally. Remove bone and meat from broth, refrigerate meat, and discard bone. Cool and refrigerate broth.

The next day, remove hardened fat from broth and discard. Place broth in large stockpot or saucepot.

5 stalks celery
1 small head cabbage
5 medium-size carrots, peeled
1 large potato, peeled
1 large onion, peeled
1 large turnip, peeled
1 (1-pound) can tomatoes, undrained (low-sodium, if desired)

3 tablespoons chopped parsley
Freshly ground black pepper
4 cups water
1 cup beef bouillon (low-sodium, if desired)
Grated Parmesan cheese (optional)

48 ⅙ ⅙ ⅙ SOUPS

With steel knife in place, chop first 6 ingredients coarsely, emptying bowl into stockpot with beef broth. Add remaining ingredients (except cheese). Bring to a boil and simmer, covered, for 1 hour. Add reserved beef and simmer another 15 minutes. Check for seasoning and serve sprinkled with grated Parmesan cheese, if desired.

This is a hearty soup and needs only some allowable crackers or toast and some fresh fruit to make a delicious lunch or light supper.

SERVES 6 TO 8

LETTUCE SOUP

Iceberg, crisphead, or head lettuce—by whatever name, a nice fresh head makes delicious soup.

*1 medium-size head iceberg
  lettuce*
1 medium-size onion, peeled
1 medium-size carrot, peeled
1 medium-size potato, peeled
3 tablespoons oil
*2 cups chicken bouillon
  (low-sodium, if desired)*
*1½ cups skim milk mixed with
  1 cup dry skim milk, or 1½
  cups evaporated skim milk*

*Pinch of curry powder
  (optional)*
*Salt (if allowed) or salt
  substitute to taste, or omit*
Pinch of sugar (or substitute)
1 teaspoon lemon juice
*Chopped mint or scallions for
  garnish*

With shredding disc in place, cut lettuce into sections to fit feed tube and shred, using medium pressure. Set aside.

Shred onion, carrot, and potato. Heat oil in large skillet and add shredded lettuce and vegetables. Sauté over medium heat, stirring constantly, for 5 minutes. Add bouillon, bring to a boil, and simmer, covered, for 5 minutes.

With steel knife in place, purée mixture in batches. Return to skillet. Add milk, seasonings, sugar, and lemon juice and heat just to boiling.

This soup is delicious served hot or chilled, and sprinkled with chopped mint or scallions.

SERVES 4 TO 6

LENTIL SOUP

Lentils are one of the oldest known legumes, and lentil soup was the "mess of pottage" for which Esau exchanged his birthright. The consensus of anyone eating a good lentil soup is that Esau gave his birthright up for a very fine meal.

1 pound dried lentils
1 clove garlic
2 large onions, peeled and
   quartered
2 large carrots, peeled and cut
   into 1-inch pieces
3 stalks celery, cut into 1-inch
   pieces
½ cup parsley sprigs
1 large potato, peeled
3 cups bouillon (low-sodium, if
   desired)

3 cups water
Salt (if allowed) or salt
   substitute, or omit
Freshly ground black pepper
1 or 2 tablespoons dry sherry,
   or to taste (optional)
Imitation bacon bits, made from
   soy protein (optional), for
   garnish

Prepare lentils as package directs. Reserve.

With steel knife in place and with machine running, drop garlic clove through feed tube and mince. Chop vegetables in order given, emptying processor bowl into large saucepot. Add bouillon, water, and lentils. Bring to a boil, cover, and simmer for 2 hours.

With steel knife in place, purée the soup in several batches and return to saucepot. If soup seems too thick, add more bouillon or water. Season to taste with salt (if used) and pepper.

Just before serving, add sherry and sprinkle with the bacon bits. This recipe replaces, most satisfactorily, those calling for a meaty ham bone.

SERVES 6 TO 8

ALLOWABLE VICHYSSOISE

A wonderful soup without the heavy cream, and tasting equally good hot or cold. The original recipe, created by the late Louis Diat, the great chef of the Ritz-Carlton Hotel in New York, is a favorite world-wide.

2 leeks
1 small onion, peeled
2 medium-size potatoes, peeled
3 tablespoons oil or margarine
2 cups chicken bouillon
  (low-sodium, if desired)

Salt (if allowed) or salt
  substitute, or omit
Freshly ground black pepper
1 cup skim milk mixed with ½
  cup dry skim milk
Chopped chives for garnish

Clean leeks. Trim root ends and cut off tops, leaving some green. Split to about ¼ inch from root end and wash thoroughly.

With slicing disc in place, slice the leeks, onion, and potatoes. In heavy saucepan, heat oil or margarine and sauté the sliced vegetables over medium heat for about 10 minutes. Add chicken bouillon and seasoning to taste. Bring to a boil, cover, and simmer gently for 30 minutes.

With steel knife in place, purée the vegetables in batches and return to saucepan. Add milk and heat through. Serve warm or chill thoroughly before serving, and sprinkle with chopped chives.

Note: If soup is too thick, add additional skim milk.

SERVES 4 TO 6

EASY SWEET POTATO SOUP

1 pound sweet potatoes (3 medium-size)
2 cups chicken bouillon (low-sodium, if desired)
Pinch of sugar (or substitute)

Nutmeg and cloves, to taste
1 cup skim milk mixed with ½ cup dry skim milk, or 1 cup evaporated skim milk
Yogurt (optional)

Peel sweet potatoes and cut into small chunks. Put in saucepan with chicken bouillon, bring to a boil, cover, and simmer until tender—about 20 minutes.

With steel knife in place, purée mixture in batches. Return to saucepan and add seasonings and milk. Heat just to boiling if serving hot.

This is also delicious cold, served with a dollop of yogurt.

SERVES 4 TO 6

CUCUMBER SOUP—Hot

½ cup parsley sprigs
(about)—to make ¼ cup
chopped
3 medium-size cucumbers,
seeded but not peeled
1 medium-size potato, peeled
1 bunch scallions, with some
green parts

3 cups chicken bouillon
(low-sodium, if desired)
¼ teaspoon dried savory
(optional)
White pepper
½ cup plain low-fat yogurt or
evaporated skim milk
Chopped parsley for garnish

With steel knife in place, add the ½ cup parsley sprigs to the
work bowl. Turn machine on and off until finely chopped. Set
aside.

With slicing disc in place, slice cucumbers, potato, and scallions, emptying bowl into large saucepan. Add reserved parsley,
bouillon, and savory. Bring to a boil, cover, and simmer for 20
minutes.

With steel knife in place, purée mixture in batches and return
to saucepan to keep warm. Just before serving, season with white
pepper to taste and stir in yogurt or milk.

Serve sprinkled with additional chopped parsley.

SERVES 4 TO 6

A COLD-DAY OATMEAL SOUP

---

*1 medium-size onion, peeled
and halved*
½ cup oatmeal
*3 cups chicken bouillon
(low-sodium, if desired)*
*Seasoning: pinch of savory or
sage or rosemary or bay
leaf—your choice*

*Salt (if allowed) or salt
substitute, or omit*
Freshly ground black pepper
*1 cup skim milk mixed with ½
cup dried skim milk*
*Chopped parsley or chives for
garnish*

With slicing disc in place, slice onion. In heavy saucepan, add onion, oatmeal, bouillon, and seasonings to taste. Bring to a boil and simmer, covered, for 1 hour.

With steel knife in place, purée the mixture in batches until smooth. Return to saucepan and add milk. Heat through, adjust seasonings, and serve hot sprinkled with some chopped parsley or chives.

Variation: Cook onion and oatmeal in chicken bouillon without further seasonings. After puréeing mixture, add 1 tablespoon sugar, a little grated nutmeg, and 1 tablespoon brandy, or to taste. A completely different taste and delicious.

SERVES 4

BROCCOLI SOUP—Cold

4 scallions, with some green
   parts
1 stalk celery, cut into 1-inch
   pieces
1 large carrot, peeled, cut into
   1-inch pieces
1 (10-ounce) package frozen
   chopped broccoli
¾ cup water
2 cups chicken bouillon
   (low-sodium, if desired)

1 cup skim milk mixed with ½
   cup dry skim milk, or 1 cup
   evaporated skim milk
Salt (if allowed) or salt
   substitute, or omit
Freshly ground black pepper
Chopped parsley or chives for
   garnish

With steel knife in place, add scallions, celery, and carrot and chop coarsely, turning machine on and off until desired consistency is reached. Add mixture to heavy saucepan with broccoli and water. Bring to a boil, cover, and simmer until tender (about 8 to 10 minutes).

With steel knife still in place, purée vegetable mixture, in 2 batches if necessary. Return to saucepan. Add chicken bouillon and simmer, covered, for 3 minutes. Remove from heat, add milk, and season to taste. Chill thoroughly for at least 3 hours before serving. Serve sprinkled with chopped parsley or chives.

To vary the flavor, add a pinch of oregano, marjoram, savory, or thyme.

SERVES 4 TO 6

CHILLED TOMATO SOUP

3 fresh ripe tomatoes, peeled,
  seeded, and quartered
1 teaspoon lemon juice
¼ teaspoon basil
¼ teaspoon celery seed

¼ teaspoon salt (if allowed) or
  salt substitute, or omit
1 cup plain low-fat yogurt
Chopped parsley or chives for
  garnish

With steel knife in place, add tomatoes, lemon juice, and seasonings. Turn machine on and off, then blend until smooth. Add yogurt, turning machine on and off until well mixed.

Chill thoroughly for at least 1 hour. Serve topped with chopped parsley or chives.

SERVES 4

CUCUMBER SOUP—Cold

There are endless varieties of cucumber soup. We find this version delicious and refreshing.

3 medium-size cucumbers,
  peeled and seeded
1 small onion, peeled and
  quartered
½ cup water
1 tablespoon white wine
  vinegar
1 teaspoon dried dill weed
1 tablespoon margarine, melted

2 cups chicken bouillon
  (low-sodium, if desired)
Salt (if allowed) or salt
  substitute, or omit
White pepper
1 (8-ounce) container plain
  low-fat yogurt
Chopped parsley, chives, or dill
  for garnish

With steel knife in place, chop cucumbers and onion coarsely, turning machine on and off for desired consistency. Add to heavy saucepan with water, vinegar, and dill weed. Bring to a boil, cover, and simmer until onion is tender (about 10 to 12 minutes).

With steel knife in place, purée the mixture until smooth. If necessary, do it in 2 batches. Empty into large bowl and stir in margarine and chicken bouillon. Season to taste and stir in yogurt. Chill thoroughly for at least 3 hours and serve garnished with parsley, chives, or dill.

SERVES 6

BORSCH, BORSHCH, BORTSCH, OR BORSCHT
(the easy way, in the food processor)

---

1 (1-pound) can sliced beets
 ,with liquid
2 tablespoons grated onion
1½ cups beef bouillon
 (low-sodium, if desired)
1 tablespoon tarragon vinegar
 (or other)

1 tablespoon lemon juice
Freshly ground black pepper to
 taste
Plain low-fat yogurt

Drain beets, reserving liquid. With steel knife in place, add beets and purée until smooth. Remove steel knife and insert shredding disc. Shred enough onion to make 2 tablespoons.

In heavy saucepan, combine beet-onion mixture with reserved beet liquid and remaining ingredients, except yogurt. Heat through, stirring frequently.

This is good served warm topped with dollops of yogurt, or chilled (for at least 3 hours) and topped with dollops of yogurt.

SERVES 4

REFRESHING SUMMER BOUILLON

1 small lemon
1 envelope (1 tablespoon) unflavored gelatin
1 envelope beef bouillon granules or 1 beef bouillon cube (low-sodium, if desired)

1 cup boiling water
1 cup cocktail vegetable juice (low-sodium, if desired)
⅓ cup good dry sherry
1 tablespoon lemon juice
Chopped parsley or chives for garnish

Cut ends of lemon flat. With slicing disc in place, insert lemon in feed tube, flat side down. If too large to insert through top, turn cover over and insert lemon through bottom of the feed tube. Slice, using medium pressure on pusher. Set aside. Wipe bowl with paper towel.

With steel knife in place, put gelatin and beef bouillon in bowl. Add boiling water and whirl until gelatin and bouillon are dissolved. Add remaining ingredients, except parsley or chives, and turn machine on and off to blend.

Pour into lightly oiled 8-inch-square pan and chill until firm, at least 3 hours. To serve, cut into small squares and pile lightly in soup cups or other attractive serving cups. Top each serving with a reserved lemon slice and chopped parsley or chives.

SERVES 4

COLD MELON SOUP

1 large ripe cantaloupe or other
  sweet melon (honeydew or
  crenshaw)
½ teaspoon (or to taste)
  powdered cinnamon or
  ginger or nutmeg or
  mace—all good

2¼ cups orange juice
2 tablespoons lemon or lime
  juice
Chopped fresh mint or mint
  sprigs for garnish

Remove rind and seeds from melon and cut into 1½-inch chunks. With steel knife in place, add melon (about 1½ cups at a time) and purée until smooth. Empty into large bowl. Add spice to last batch in food processor and process with the melon.

Add orange juice and lemon or lime juice to purée in bowl, mix well, and chill thoroughly for at least 1 hour.

Serve sprinkled with some chopped fresh mint or a mint sprig.

SERVES 4 TO 6

CHILLED FRUIT SOUP

1 pound ripe apricots, plums, or
  peaches
1 tablespoon lemon juice
1 quart water
Sugar (or sugar substitute) to
  taste

¼ cup dry white wine or
  sherry, to taste (or sweet
  wine, if preferred)
Plain low-fat yogurt
Cinnamon or nutmeg
  (optional)

Wash and pit the fruit and place in heavy saucepan with lemon juice and water. Bring to a boil, cover, and simmer until fruit is very tender.

With steel knife in place, purée fruit mixture in batches and return to saucepan. Add sugar to taste—you won't need much if fruit is ripe—and the wine or sherry and stir over low heat until sugar is dissolved.

Chill thoroughly for at least 3 hours and serve with a dollop of yogurt.

Try adding a little cinnamon or nutmeg for additional flavor.

SERVES 4 TO 6

SUMMER PEA SOUP

½ teaspoon fresh mint or ¼ teaspoon dried
1 small onion, peeled
1 medium-size carrot, peeled
1 (10-ounce) package frozen peas
2 cups chicken bouillon (low-sodium, if desired)

Dash of sugar
Dash of nutmeg
1½ cups skim milk mixed with ½ cup dry skim milk, or 1½ cups evaporated skim milk
Salt (if allowed) or salt substitute, or omit
Mint sprigs for garnish

With steel knife in place, chop mint, turning machine on and off until finely minced. Set aside.

With shredding disc in place, shred onion and carrot and add to heavy saucepan with reserved mint, peas, bouillon, sugar, and nutmeg. Bring to a boil, cover, and simmer about 30 minutes.

With steel knife in place, purée mixture in batches until

smooth, emptying into large bowl. Stir in milk and season to taste. Chill well for at least 3 hours. Top each serving with a mint sprig.

SERVES **4** TO **6**

SUMMER STRAWBERRY SOUP

---

*1 quart ripe strawberries,
  washed and hulled*
1½ cups water
*½ cup sugar (use half sugar
  substitute, if desired)*

1 tablespoon lemon juice
1 tablespoon minute tapioca
*½ cup dry white wine
  (optional but delicious)*

With steel knife in place, purée strawberries in batches—1½ cups at a time. Remove to heavy saucepan and add remaining ingredients except wine. Bring to a boil and simmer gently, uncovered and stirring often, for 15 minutes. Remove from heat and add white wine. Chill thoroughly for at least 3 hours.

SERVES **4** TO **6**

BEEF STOCK—Low-sodium

After making the stock, freeze it in cubes, in cups, or in whatever quantities you will be using most frequently.

*3 pounds beef shin (have the
  butcher crack bone)*

1 tablespoon oil
2½ quarts water

Trim the meat from the bones and cut into small pieces. In large kettle, heat oil and brown meat and bones very lightly. Add water, heat to boiling, and simmer, covered, for 4 hours. Skim from time to time.

1 medium-size onion, peeled and quartered	2 stalks celery, with tops, cut into 1-inch pieces
2 medium-size carrots, peeled and cut into 1-inch pieces	6 whole peppercorns
	3 sprigs parsley, with stems

After meat has simmered for almost 4 hours, with steel knife in place, coarsely chop onion, carrots, and celery. Add vegetables, peppercorns, and parsley to large kettle and simmer 1 hour more.

When cool enough to handle, strain stock through a *fine* sieve or colander. Discard meat, bones, and vegetables. Chill stock for several hours, or until fat has risen to top and can be removed. Stock is now ready to use in any recipe calling for beef broth or bouillon, or it may be frozen.

If you wish to clarify the stock, add a slightly beaten egg white and broken egg shell to strained, cold stock. Bring to a boil, stirring constantly. Remove from heat, let cool, and strain through double thickness of cheesecloth.

MAKES ABOUT 2 QUARTS

CHICKEN STOCK—Low-sodium

Follow same procedure as for the preceding Beef Stock, using about 3 pounds of chicken. Cook chicken pieces for 3 hours before adding vegetables. Strain, chill, and remove all fat before using or freezing.

Salvage the cooked chicken to use in salads or sandwiches.

MAKES ABOUT 2 QUARTS

Salads and
Salad Dressings

About Salads and Salad Dressings

Salads take many forms, and the choice of ingredients is endless. With the help of the food processor, slicing, shredding, and chopping vegetables and fruits for salads are quick and almost effortless.

The following recipes are only a small sample of the unlimited combination of ingredients that can be used in salad making. Included are the simplest of salads, using a minimum of ingredients to complement the meal, to main-dish salads that *are* the meal.

Use your food processor to make your own fresh salad dressings and mayonnaise in a matter of seconds. The flavor is outstanding and you know all the ingredients are allowable.

CHICKEN LUNCHEON SALAD

*2 whole chicken breasts,
  poached (see index), or 3½
  cups leftover boneless,
  skinless chicken*
*1 teaspoon grated orange rind
  (3 strips orange zest)*
¼ cup sugar (or substitute)
2 medium-size stalks celery
4 to 5 scallions, white part only
*Salt (if allowed) or salt
  substitute, or omit*

1 tablespoon lemon juice
*1 small can (about 9 ounces)
  pineapple tidbits packed in
  natural juice, drained*
*½ cup slivered almonds,
  toasted (optional, but good)*
½ cup mayonnaise (see index)
Salad greens
*Mandarin orange slices for
  garnish (optional)*

Cut chicken into cubes and place in large bowl.

With steel knife in place, cut orange zest into pieces and add to food processor bowl with sugar. Turn machine on and off, then let run until zest is finely minced. Set aside.

With slicing disc in place, slice celery and scallions and add to chicken. Sprinkle chicken with salt (if used) to taste and lemon juice and combine gently.

Just before serving, fold in pineapple tidbits and almonds. Mix reserved orange rind-sugar mixture with mayonnaise and carefully fold into chicken mixture. Serve on greens, garnished with mandarin orange slices, if desired.

SERVES 4 TO 6

EASY CHICKEN SALAD

1/3 cup firmly packed parsley

3 stalks celery, cut into 1-inch pieces

1/2 cup low-fat, creamed cottage cheese

2 cups cooked chicken breast, skinned, boned, and cut into chunks

1/2 cup mayonnaise (see index)

Salt (if allowed) or salt substitute to taste, or omit

Freshly ground black pepper to taste

Salad greens

With steel knife in place, chop parsley. Add celery and turn machine on and off just until coarsely chopped. Add cottage cheese and turn machine on and off. Add remaining ingredients and turn machine on and off, until chicken is coarsely chopped. You may have to scrape down bowl. Serve on salad greens.

Variations: Add a pinch of tarragon or curry powder to taste. Or add chopped walnuts or almonds. Or add an apple, peeled, seeded, and chopped.

SERVES 4

MAIN-DISH RICE SALAD

1 cup uncooked rice (not instant)

¼ cup oil

1 tablespoon lemon juice or vinegar

Salt (if allowed) or salt substitute, or omit

Freshly ground black pepper

½ cup parsley leaves

5 scallions, with some green parts

2 medium-size stalks celery

8 radishes

¼ pound fresh mushrooms

2 cups cooked chicken breast, skinned, boned, and cut into cubes

½ cup mayonnaise (see index) mixed with 1 tablespoon lemon juice

Salad greens

Cucumber slices for garnish

Cherry tomatoes for garnish

Cook rice according to package directions. In large bowl, toss rice with oil, lemon juice or vinegar, and salt (if used) and pepper to taste. Cool slightly.

With steel knife in place, mince parsley, turning machine on and off. Then with machine running, drop scallions through feed tube and mince fine. Set mixture aside.

With slicing disc in place, slice celery, radishes, and mushrooms. Add vegetables, reserved parsley-scallion mixture, and chicken to rice and toss gently. Chill thoroughly for at least 2 hours. Just before serving, combine mayonnaise and lemon juice and fold into salad. Serve on salad greens and garnish with cucumber slices and cherry tomatoes.

Variation: Use leftover beef instead of chicken.

SERVES 4 TO 6

VEGETABLE SALAD

With the food processor able to slice and shred vegetables so quickly, combinations of vegetables usually eaten cooked are attractive and delicious served in their raw state, chilled. In the following recipe, the green beans are blanched—they have a better texture for a chilled salad.

½ pound fresh green beans, blanched and french-cut
2 zucchini
3 scallions, white part only
2 stalks celery
4 to 6 nice fresh mushrooms

Salt (if allowed) or salt substitute, or omit
Freshly ground black pepper
Oil and wine vinegar
Mayonnaise (see index)

The beans should be chilled before slicing, so after trimming ends and cutting them into lengths to fit crosswise in feed tube, drop them into boiling water for about 8 minutes. Plunge into cold water, than drain well and refrigerate for several hours.

With slicing disc in place, pack feed tube full of green beans, making certain they are crosswise. Use gentle pressure on pusher and "french" the beans. Repeat as necessary and remove to large bowl. Slice zucchini, scallions, and celery, removing to bowl with beans. Line up mushrooms in feed tube and slice, adding to other vegetables.

Season with salt (if used)and freshly ground pepper to taste, and dress with just enough oil and vinegar to moisten. Chill well. Just before serving, toss with a tablespoon or two of mayonnaise.

SERVES 4

COLD FROSTED CAULIFLOWER

Avocados are not generally recommended on a strict low-cholesterol diet. However, the amount per serving is small and the salad delicious.

1 medium-size head cauliflower
1 tablespoon finely minced
   onion or scallions, white part
   only
¼ cup wine vinegar
¾ cup oil
Salt (if allowed) or salt
   substitute, or omit
Freshly ground black pepper

Garlic powder (optional)
1 ripe avocado, peeled, pitted
1 teaspoon lemon juice
½ cup mayonnaise (see index)
1 teaspoon dried dill weed
Green food coloring (optional)
Dried dill weed, chopped fresh
   dill, or chopped parsley for
   garnish

Cook cauliflower whole, in boiling water, until just tender-crisp. Drain well and place, core side down, in deep bowl.

With steel knife in place, mince onion or scallions. Add vinegar, oil, and seasonings to taste and turn machine on and off to blend. Pour mixture over cooked cauliflower and let marinate for at least 1 hour.

With steel knife in place, chunk avocado and add to bowl with lemon juice. Turn machine on and off, then let run until smooth. Add mayonnaise and dill weed and turn machine on and off to mix well. (For more color, try a drop of green food coloring.)

When ready to serve, remove cauliflower from marinade and frost with avocado mixture. Sprinkle with additional dried dill weed, chopped fresh dill, or chopped parsley.

Variation: Instead of using avocado, increase mayonnaise to ⅔ cup and add ¼ cup chili sauce or catsup (low-sodium, if desired). This will give you a rosy cauliflower instead of a green one.

SERVES 6 TO 8

REFRESHING CHEESE-CUCUMBER SALAD

½ cup parsley sprigs
2 medium-size cucumbers,
  peeled and seeded
8 ounces low-fat creamed
  cottage cheese
Salt (if allowed) or salt
  substitute, or omit

2 teaspoons lemon juice—more
  if desired
Salad greens
Grapefruit and/or orange
  sections for garnish

With steel knife in place, mince parsley and set aside.

With shredding disc in place, cut cucumbers to fit feed tube and shred. Set aside to drain well. Reinsert steel knife and add cottage cheese, salt (if used) to taste, lemon juice, and reserved minced parsley. Turn machine on and off to mix well. Add drained cucumbers and turn machine on and off just to distribute evenly. Chill thoroughly.

Serve on salad greens surrounded with chilled grapefruit and/or orange sections.

SERVES 4 TO 6

FRESH CUCUMBER MOUSSE

This is also delicious as an hors d'oeuvre with Melba rounds.

1 cup evaporated skim milk,
   well chilled

2 medium-size cucumbers,
   peeled and seeded

1 envelope (1 tablespoon)
   unflavored gelatin

⅓ cup boiling water

3 to 4 scallions, white part only

½ cup mayonnaise (see index)

1 tablespoon prepared
   horseradish (low-sodium, if
   desired)

Salt (if allowed) or salt
   substitute, or omit

White pepper

Watercress or parsley sprigs for
   garnish

Mayonnaise (optional)

Place milk in freezer so it will be very cold—a few ice crystals will make it even better.

Cut cucumbers in chunks and with steel knife in place turn machine on and off until cucumbers are puréed. You will need 1½ cups. Set aside.

Empty gelatin into work bowl. Add boiling water and scallions. Blend, turning machine on and off until scallions are liquefied. Add the ½ cup mayonnaise, the horseradish, and seasonings to taste. Turn machine on and off to mix. Add reserved cucumbers and turn machine on and off to mix. Pour in chilled milk and let machine run for 20 seconds.

Oil a 4-cup mold. Pour mixture into mold and refrigerate until firm, about 3 to 4 hours. To serve, unmold onto serving plate and surround with watercress or parsley sprigs. Pass additional mayonnaise, if desired.

SERVES 6

JUST A CUCUMBER SALAD

There are countless ways of presenting sliced cucumbers—almost every one refreshing and delicious. Below are some suggestions for this diet that are both simple and tasty.

From 1 large cucumber you get approximately 1½ cups slices. This will serve 2 to 3 people as a salad, so you can add or subtract depending upon the number you are serving. In addition to the sliced cucumbers, you need only your choice of dressing.

Cut ends off cucumbers and peel or not, as desired. Cut in lengths to fit feed tube and, with slicing disc in place, slice as many as you need. Place in slightly salted water for 30 minutes, then drain thoroughly, or place in plain ice water (this will produce a crisper cucumber) for 30 minutes and drain thoroughly. You can eliminate the soaking altogether and mix immediately with the dressing, but the cucumbers will tend to be more watery and not as crisp.

Suggested dressings:

OIL AND VINEGAR DRESSING

2 tablespoons oil
2 tablespoons vinegar
Salt (if allowed) or salt
    substitute to taste, or omit

*Freshly ground black pepper to
    taste*
⅛ *teaspoon dried dill weed*

Mix all ingredients with cucumbers and chill before serving. (This quantity of dressing is enough for 1½ cups sliced cucumbers.)

SERVES 2 TO 3

MOCK SOUR CREAM DRESSING

1 cup plain low-fat yogurt
2 tablespoons wine vinegar
Dash of sugar (or substitute)

Dash of garlic powder
¼ cup oil

With plastic or steel knife in place, combine ingredients and pour over drained cucumbers. Mix and chill.

MAKES 1 CUP

YOGURT DRESSING

1 teaspoon fresh mint or ½
teaspoon dried
1 cup plain low-fat yogurt

Dash of sugar (or substitute)
Dash of garlic powder

With steel knife in place, add mint and chop fine. Add remaining ingredients and turn machine on and off to mix. Pour over drained cucumbers, mix, and chill.

MAKES 1 CUP

Variation: Add some orange and grapefruit sections to the cucumbers. Delicious with the Yogurt Dressing.

1 LARGE CUCUMBER SERVES 2 TO 3

LEMON-CUCUMBER SALAD

1 (4-ounce) package
low-calorie lemon-flavor
gelatin
1 cup hot water
1 tablespoon lemon juice
1 tablespoon white vinegar
2 large cucumbers, peeled and
seeded

1 tablespoon chopped fresh dill
or 1½ teaspoons dried dill
weed
Watercress
Plain low-fat yogurt
Chopped chives or fresh dill
sprigs for garnish

Dissolve gelatin in hot water. Add lemon juice and vinegar and chill until mixture begins to set.

With shredding disc in place, cut cucumbers into lengths to fit crosswise in feed tube. Shred cucumbers and drain well.

When gelatin is partially set, stir in cucumbers and chopped dill. Pour into lightly oiled 8-inch-square pan and chill until firm, about 3 to 4 hours.

To serve, cut into small cubes and pile into attractive glass dishes lined with watercress. Top each serving with a dollop of plain low-fat yogurt and sprinkle with chopped chives or a dill sprig.

SERVES 4 TO 6

GREEN PEA SALAD

2 (10-ounce) packages frozen
  peas (petite recommended)
1 cup beef bouillon
  (low-sodium, if desired)
1 stalk celery
6 to 8 water chestnuts
4 tablespoons vinegar

2 tablespoons oil
¼ teaspoon dried mint, crushed
Freshly ground pepper
½ cup plain low-fat yogurt
Lettuce
Sliced tomatoes for garnish

Cook peas in beef bouillon, according to package directions. Drain, reserving ½ cup of cooking liquid. Place peas in deep bowl.

With slicing disc in place, slice celery and water chestnuts and add to peas.

With plastic or steel knife in place, add reserved cooking liquid, vinegar, oil, mint, and pepper to taste. Turn machine on and off to mix well. Pour over vegetables and mix gently. Chill thoroughly for several hours or overnight.

Just before serving, mix in yogurt. Serve in lettuce-lined bowl surrounded by sliced tomatoes.

SERVES 6

MUSHROOM AND RADISH SALAD

Simple, delicious, low calorie, and easily prepared in the food processor.

½ pound fresh mushrooms

1 bunch radishes, trimmed

2 tablespoons lemon juice or
vinegar

½ cup oil

Salt (if allowed) or salt
substitute to taste, or omit

Freshly ground black pepper to
taste

Chopped parsley or chives for
garnish

With slicing disc in place, fill feed tube with mushrooms and slice. Repeat, and set aside in mixing bowl. Slice radishes and add to mushrooms.

With plastic or steel knife in place, add remaining ingredients, except garnish, and turn machine on and off to blend. Pour over mushrooms and radishes and mix well. Chill for at least 1 hour and serve sprinkled with chopped parsley or chives.

SERVES 3 TO 4

RED AND WHITE RADISH SALAD

⅓ cup parsley sprigs

1 bunch red radishes, trimmed

1 bunch white radishes,
trimmed

½ cup shredded carrot
(1 medium-size)

½ cup plain low-fat yogurt

1 teaspoon sugar (or substitute)

Salt (if allowed) or salt
substitute, or omit

Lettuce

With steel knife in place, mince parsley. Set aside.

With slicing disc in place, fill feed tube with red and white radishes and slice, repeating until all are sliced, emptying into large mixing bowl.

With shredding disc in place, cut carrot to fit crosswise in feed tube and shred. Add to radishes, reserving a few for garnish.

Mix radishes and carrots with yogurt, sugar, and salt (if used) to taste. Chill thoroughly for at least 1 hour. To serve, arrange on lettuce-lined plates and garnish with reserved carrot shreds and chopped parsley.

SERVES 6

SALADE COMPOSÉE

With the food processor, a *salad composée* is easy, eye-appealing, and delicious. The term means "arranged salad": each vegetable or fruit is individually placed on the serving dish, and the salad is artfully garnished, creating a picture in color, design, and texture. Try the following combination or "compose" your own.

1 cup parsley sprigs
½ small head cabbage
4 medium-size carrots, peeled
4 medium-size turnips, peeled
½ cup sliced radishes or ½ cup pitted, sliced ripe olives
1 lemon

½ cup oil
2 tablespoons lemon juice
1 teaspoon dried dill weed
Salt (if allowed) or salt substitute to taste, or omit
Freshly ground black pepper to taste

Have ready a large, shallow serving dish. With steel knife in place, add parsley. Turn machine on and off, then let run until finely minced. Set aside.

With shredding disc in place, shred cabbage, carrots, and turnips separately and arrange them side by side on the large dish with the carrots in the center.

With slicing disc in place, slice enough radishes (or olives) to make ½ cup. Set aside. Slice lemon. Cut ends flat and, if too large to fit through top of feed tube, insert from bottom.

Make rows of sliced radishes or olives between the vegetables on the large dish. Cut lemon slices in half and tuck them around the rim of the serving dish. Sprinkle reserved parsley around the edge, leaving lemon rims visible.

With plastic or steel knife in place, mix remaining ingredients. Just before serving, drizzle over salad.

SERVES 6 TO 8

TOMATO-CHEESE ASPIC SALAD

¼ cup parsley sprigs
1 envelope (1 tablespoon)
   unflavored gelatin
½ cup boiling water
1 teaspoon lemon juice
4 scallions, white part only
¼ cup mayonnaise (see index)
1½ cups low-fat creamed
   cottage cheese

½ cup tomato juice
   (low-sodium, if desired)
¼ cup tomato sauce
   (low-sodium, if desired)
½ teaspoon celery seed
Cucumber slices or zucchini
   and carrot sticks

With steel knife in place, chop parsley and set aside.

Empty gelatin into work bowl and add boiling water, lemon juice, and scallions. Turn machine on and off and let run until scallions are liquefied. Add mayonnaise and cottage cheese and blend until smooth. Add tomato juice, tomato sauce, celery seed, and reserved parsley. Turn machine on and off to blend well.

Pour into oiled 4-cup mold and refrigerate until firm, at least 3 to 4 hours.

To serve, unmold onto serving plate and surround with cucumber slices or zucchini and carrot sticks (use the french fry disc).

SERVES 6 TO 8

CITRUS-COTTAGE CHEESE MOLD

1 cup sliced seedless grapes or
fresh strawberries
1½ cups low-fat creamed
cottage cheese
1½ envelopes (1½
tablespoons) unflavored
gelatin

⅔ cup orange juice
1 cup boiling water
¼ cup sugar (or substitute)
¼ cup lemon juice
Salad greens
Fresh fruits

With slicing disc in place, fill feed tube with grapes or strawberries and slice, using light pressure. Repeat until you have 1 cup fruit. Set aside in refrigerator.

With steel knife in place, add cottage cheese and process until completely smooth. Set aside.

Add gelatin to bowl with orange juice. Let sit a few minutes to soften. Add boiling water, sugar, and lemon juice. Turn machine on and off, then let run for 4 seconds to dissolve gelatin.

Add reserved cottage cheese and turn machine on and off to incorporate. Remove bowl from processor base with steel knife in place and refrigerate entire unit until mixture thickens.

Return bowl to processor base, making certain steel knife is in position on shaft. Turn machine on and off 3 times, using 3- to 4-second bursts.

Fold in grapes or strawberries and turn into oiled 4-cup mold. Chill until firm, at least 3 to 4 hours. Unmold onto salad greens and serve with additional fresh fruits.

Use a combination of grapes and strawberries in basic recipe—delicious.

SERVES 6

TURNIPS RAW

Many vegetables are delicious in their raw state. Vegetables raw not only "develop the jaw," as Ogden Nash once noted when referring to celery, but are beneficial to us in many other ways, particularly on this diet. And the food processor, with its slicing, shredding, and chopping capabilities, facilitates the preparation of the vegetables raw.

2 pounds turnips, peeled
2 tablespoons toasted sesame
  seeds
4 scallions, white part only
½ cup mayonnaise (see index)
½ cup plain low-fat yogurt

Salt (if allowed) or salt
  substitute to taste, or omit
Freshly ground black pepper to
  taste
Minced parsley for garnish

Using the french fry disc or the shredding disc, cut turnips to fit crosswise in feed tube and process, emptying work bowl into large salad bowl.

To toast sesame seeds, preheat oven to 350° F. Spread seeds in pie pan and brown in oven. Let cool.

With steel knife in place, and with machine running, drop scallions through feed tube and mince, turning machine on and off. Add remaining ingredients except parsley and turn machine on and off to mix well. If you aren't going to use the dressing immediately, wait and add the sesame seeds just before you mix the dressing with the turnips. Serve sprinkled with parsley.

Experiment with other herbs and spices in the dressing—a pinch of tarragon, nutmeg, or curry powder.

SERVES 6 TO 8

WALDORF SALAD
WITH AN OPTIONAL DIFFERENCE

½ cup walnuts
3 medium-size stalks celery
1½ medium-size red Delicious apples, peeled and cored
½ medium-size red Delicious apple, cored

Lemon juice
½ cup mayonnaise (see index)
Salt (if allowed) or salt substitute, or omit
1 teaspoon lemon juice

With steel knife in place, chop walnuts coarsely. Set aside in large salad bowl.

With slicing disc in place, slice celery and apples. Reserve unpeeled slices for garnish and sprinkle with lemon juice to prevent their turning brown before serving. Add peeled apple slices and celery to walnuts.

Combine mayonnaise, salt (if used) to taste, and the 1 teaspoon lemon juice and mix with apples, celery, and walnuts. Serve garnished wih reserved apple slices.

The optional difference: To the above salad mixture, add about 2 cups cooked fresh or frozen crab meat or shrimp and serve with lemon wedges. Shellfish, at one time, was a real feature in coronary cuisine. It contains almost no fat. However, it has since been discovered that what fat it does contain is almost all cholesterol. Some of the frozen and most of the canned shellfish is also high in sodium content. Now and then a moderate serving of shellfish is a good change of pace for the dieter and makes the otherwise ordinary Waldorf Salad a dish with a delightful difference.

SERVES 4 TO 6

CABBAGE SALAD

---

1 clove garlic, peeled (optional)
1 small onion, peeled and
quartered
1 small green pepper, seeded
and quartered
½ medium-size head cabbage
3 small carrots, peeled

2 stalks celery
Freshly ground black pepper
⅛ to ¼ teaspoon dried
oregano, or to taste
5 tablespoons oil
1 tablespoon vinegar

With steel knife in place and with machine running, drop garlic through feed tube. Turn machine on and off to mince. Add onion and green pepper and turn on and off until coarsely chopped. Set mixture aside in large bowl.

With shredding disc in place cut cabbage into wedges to fit

feed tube. Shred cabbage and carrots and add to bowl with onion-green pepper mixture.

With slicing disc in place, slice celery and add to cabbage mixture. Sprinkle pepper and oregano to taste over vegetables. Drizzle oil and vinegar over all and toss lightly.

Variation: Add some french-cut green beans to salad before tossing. See Vegetable Salad (see index) for directions for frenching the beans.

SERVES 4 TO 6

A DIFFERENT SLAW

For a change, try celery instead of cabbage. This is a delicious slaw.

4 to 5 stalks celery
2 medium-size carrots
½ cup plain low-fat yogurt
¼ cup mayonnaise (see index)
1 tablespoon wine vinegar
1 teaspoon sugar (or substitute)
¼ teaspoon paprika

Salt (if allowed) or salt
*   substitute to taste, or omit*
1 tablespoon chopped chives
Sliced radishes and/or sliced or
*   chopped green onions for*
*   garnish*

With slicing disc in place, cut celery into lengths to fit feed tube, pack tightly, and slice. You should have about 3 cups. Turn into mixing bowl.

With shredding disc in place, shred carrots and add to celery.

With plastic or steel knife in place, add remaining ingredients, except garnish, and turn on and off until well mixed. Drizzle over celery and carrots, toss lightly, and chill thoroughly for several hours.

Serve topped with sliced radishes and/or sliced or chopped green onions.

SERVES 4 TO 6

ANOTHER SLAW

1 small head cabbage
4 small carrots, peeled
1 tart apple, peeled, cored, and
   quartered
½ cup mayonnaise (see index)
¼ cup plain low-fat yogurt

1 tablespoon poppy seeds
1 teaspoon lemon juice
Salt (if allowed) or salt
   substitute to taste, or omit
Freshly ground black pepper to
   taste

With shredding disc in place, cut cabbage into wedges to fit feed tube and shred. Empty into large mixing bowl. Shred carrots and apple and add to cabbage.

With plastic or steel knife in place, add remaining ingredients and turn machine on and off to mix well. Pour over cabbage mixture, toss lightly, and chill for several hours.

Instead of poppy seeds, try a sprinkle of caraway seeds for a different flavor.

SERVES 4 TO 6

MINTED ONION RELISH (OR SALAD)

This is delicious served with meat or as a separate salad.

4 to 5 small onions (sized to fit
   feed tube whole), peeled
2 tablespoons freshly chopped
   mint leaves or 1 tablespoon
   dried mint
⅔ cup vinegar

⅓ cup oil
½ cup sugar (or substitute)
Salt (if allowed) or substitute
   to taste, or omit
Salad greens (optional)

With slicing disc in place, insert onions, whole, in feed tube and slice, using moderate pressure. Cover onions with cold water and refrigerate overnight.

If using fresh mint, with steel knife in place, chop mint, turning machine on and off. Set aside. Combine remaining ingredients, turning machine on and off to mix.

Drain onions thoroughly. Add mint and dressing and chill again for several hours, turning mixture several times.

Serve as an accompaniment to meats or on greens as a salad.

SERVES 4 TO 6 AS A SALAD
SERVES 8 OR MORE AS A RELISH

ONION-PEPPER RELISH

Since commercial relishes and pickles are off limits in the diet as a rule, keep the following on hand. Often with chopped meats, sandwiches, or salads a relish will enhance the meal.

3 medium-size green peppers,
    seeded
6 small onions (sized to fit feed
    tube whole) peeled
Dried hot peppers (to your
    taste, but go easy)

2 cups white wine vinegar
1 cup sugar (use half granulated
    and half substitute)

With steel knife in place, chunk peppers, add to work bowl, and chop coarsely. Set aside in mixing bowl.

With slicing disc in place, cut bottom of onions flat and slice, using medium pressure. Add to peppers. Also add dried hot peppers. Cover mixture with boiling water and let stand for 10 minutes. Drain in colander.

In large saucepan, add vinegar and sugar and heat, stirring, until sugar is dissolved. Add vegetables, bring to a boil, and simmer, uncovered, for 15 minutes. Cool and store in refrigerator.

This is delicious served on top of low-fat cottage cheese as a salad.

MAKES ABOUT 3 CUPS RELISH

MAYONNAISE

Mayonnaise made in the food processor is second only to peanut butter in popularity. Both are made easily and quickly. Both are delicious. The following three basic recipes for mayonnaise were developed for this diet. If sodium restriction is a concern, skip the first recipe using egg whites.

EGG-WHITE-ONLY MAYONNAISE

1 or 2 egg whites
1 teaspoon mustard (dry or prepared)
1 teaspoon vinegar
1 tablespoon lemon juice
Dash of cayenne, if desired

Dash of salt (if allowed) or salt substitute, or omit
1 cup oil
1 tablespoon evaporated skim milk

With steel knife in place, combine first 6 ingredients plus 1 tablespoon oil in processor bowl. Turn machine on and off 3 times to mix well. Then, with machine running, pour remaining oil slowly through feed tube. When mayonnaise has thickened, add evaporated milk and turn machine on and off to incorporate well.

MAKES A LITTLE OVER 1 CUP

EGGLESS MAYONNAISE

¼ cup evaporated skim milk, chilled overnight (important)
½ teaspoon sugar (or substitute)
¼ teaspoon dry mustard
Dash of paprika

Dash of cayenne pepper
Dash of salt (if allowed) or salt substitute, or omit
1 teaspoon vinegar
1 tablespoon lemon juice
1 cup oil

With steel knife in place, combine first 8 ingredients plus 1 tablespoon oil in processor bowl. Turn machine on and off several times to thicken. Then, with machine running, pour remaining oil slowly through feed tube.

MAKES A LITTLE OVER 1 CUP

NO-EGG MAYONNAISE

3 tablespoons Fleischmann's
   Egg Beaters
Pinch of sugar, if desired (or
   substitute)
1 teaspoon lemon juice
1 teaspoon vinegar
1 teaspoon dry mustard (or
   prepared, if desired)

Pinch of salt (if allowed) or salt
   substitute, or omit
Freshly ground black pepper or
   dash of cayenne
1 cup oil

With steel knife in place, combine first 7 ingredients plus 1 tablespoon of oil in processor bowl. Turn machine on and off twice to combine ingredients. With machine running, pour remaining oil slowly through feed tube. This mayonnaise will thicken quickly. Turn machine off as soon as remaining oil has been added. This keeps well and, because it is very thick, is excellent for sandwiches or salads. Mixed with an equal amount of plain low-fat yogurt and some curry powder to taste, it is delicious on some vegetables—try asparagus, broccoli, Brussels sprouts, cabbage, cauliflower, eggplant, mushrooms, onions, squash, and tomatoes.

MAKES A LITTLE OVER 1 CUP

ITALIAN MAYONNAISE

½ small onion, peeled, or 4 to 5
   scallions, white part only
Pinch of sugar, if desired (or
   substitute)

⅛ teaspoon oregano
⅛ teaspoon thyme
⅛ teaspoon rosemary
⅛ teaspoon basil

Garlic powder (optional) to
    taste
Salt (if allowed) or salt
    substitute to taste, or omit

Freshly ground black pepper to
    taste
2 tablespoons red wine vinegar
1 cup mayonnaise (see index)

With steel knife in place, chop onion or scallions fine. Add remaining ingredients and process, turning machine on and off until well mixed. Chill before using, at least 4 hours—so that flavor can develop.

Delicious with any kind of greens or vegetable salads.

MAKES 1¼ CUPS

FRENCH MAYONNAISE

1 cup mayonnaise (see index)
1 tablespoon vinegar
1 tablespoon lemon juice
1 teaspoon dry mustard

Pinch of garlic powder
Salt (if allowed) or salt
    substitute to taste, or omit

With plastic or steel knife in place, mix all ingredients, turning machine on and off. Chill thoroughly for at least 4 hours. This is a good, creamy French dressing for vegetables and green salads.

MAKES 1 CUP

DILL-TARRAGON MAYONNAISE

This is a wonderfully flavored mayonnaise for tuna or chicken salad or sandwiches.

1 cup mayonnaise (see index)   *1 teaspoon dried tarragon*
1 teaspoon dried dill weed

With plastic or steel knife in place, combine ingredients, turning machine on and off. Refrigerate overnight to allow flavor to develop.

MAKES 1 CUP

EASY LOW-CALORIE BLEU CHEESE DRESSING

This is delicious on greens or vegetable salads.

1 (8-ounce) container low-fat   *1 tablespoon vinegar*
  cottage cheese or pot cheese   *Pinch of sugar (or substitute)*
1 tablespoon bleu cheese   *Skim milk*

With steel knife in place, add cottage cheese and bleu cheese to processor bowl. Turn machine on and off, then let whirl until completely smooth. You may have to scrape down sides. Add vinegar and sugar and blend. With machine running, add just enough skim milk to make the dressing the right consistency for pouring over salads.

MAKES 1¼ CUPS

ORANGE-CHEESE DRESSING

Delicious on plain shredded carrots or cabbage.

1 (8-ounce) container low-fat   *2 tablespoons orange juice*
cottage cheese or pot cheese   *1 tablespoon lemon juice*
2 tablespoons orange marmalade   *Skim milk*

With steel knife in place, add all ingredients except milk to processor bowl. Turn machine on and off, then let it whirl until mixture is smooth. With machine running, add just enough skim milk to make dressing desired consistency—it should be smooth and creamy.

MAKES 1¼ CUPS

REFRESHING BUTTERMILK DRESSING
FOR GREENS

---

1 small cucumber, peeled and   *⅓ cup buttermilk*
seeded   *Salt (if allowed) or salt*
3 tablespoons mayonnaise (see   *substitute to taste, or omit*
index)   *Freshly ground black pepper to*
2 tablespoons lemon juice   *taste*
½ teaspoon dried dill weed

With shredding disc in place, shred cucumber and set aside to drain well.

With plastic or steel knife in place, add remaining ingredients and turn machine on and off to mix well. Stir in drained cucumbers and chill.

MAKES ABOUT ¾ CUP DRESSING, OR ENOUGH FOR ABOUT
6 CUPS OF CRISP GREENS

Vegetables

About Vegetables

Vegetables provide an unlimited challenge for anyone with a food processor and some imagination. The choice is, of course, infinite: shredded, french-cut, sliced, chopped, or puréed, singly or in combination.

Vegetables are not restricted to side dishes in this book, although this chapter is devoted to that category. They are also found in the hors d'oeuvre, soup, salad, and main-course sections.

Anyone who must watch calories or cholesterol will find that the following recipes help rediscover the freshness and variety of vegetables without the use of butter and rich sauces.

SIMPLY SHREDDED CARROTS AND ZUCCHINI

---

3 medium-size carrots, peeled
2 medium-size zucchini,
  unpeeled
½ cup water

Freshly ground black pepper
Choice of other seasonings (see
  below)

With shredding disc in place, cut carrots and zucchini into maximum length to fit crosswise in feed tube. Shred, using medium pressure. Repeat as necessary. Empty bowl into heavy skillet.

Add water to skillet, bring to a boil, and simmer, covered, for 4 or 5 minutes, or until tender-crisp.

Drain, if necessary, and season to taste. Freshly ground pepper is enough. You can add a tablespoon of margarine, some freshly chopped parsley, and about 1 to 2 teaspoons lemon juice. Try a pinch of nutmeg or curry powder. Try a pinch of marjoram. Experiment!

SERVES 4

SIMPLY SHREDDED BEETS

1 pound fresh beets, peeled
1/3 cup water
1 tablespoon vinegar
1 tablespoon margarine

1/2 teaspoon chopped fresh dill
or 1/4 teaspoon celery seed, or
to taste

With shredding disc in place, cut beets into maximum length to fit crosswise in feed tube. Shred, using medium pressure.

In heavy saucepan or skillet, place beets, water, and vinegar. Bring to a boil and simmer, covered, for 6 to 8 minutes. Drain beets. Add margarine and seasonings.

SERVES 3 TO 4

SIMPLY SHREDDED TURNIPS

1 pound turnips, peeled
1/4 cup chicken bouillon
  (low-sodium, if desired)

Freshly ground black pepper
1/8 teaspoon dried dill weed, or
  to taste

With shredding disc in place, cut turnips into maximum length to fit crosswise in feed tube. Shred, using medium pressure.

In heavy saucepan, bring bouillon to a boil. Add turnips and simmer, covered, for 5 minutes. Drain, if necessary, and season to taste.

SERVES 3 TO 4

SIMPLY SHREDDED CABBAGE

1 small head cabbage
Margarine
Salt (if allowed) or salt
   substitute, or omit

Freshly ground black pepper
Vinegar

Core and cut cabbage into pieces to fit feed tube. With shredding disc in place, shred cabbage, using medium pressure.

Bring enough water to a boil to cover cabbage. Drop cabbage into boiling water, cover, and simmer for 5 minutes. Drain well and season with margarine, salt (if used), and pepper to taste. The cabbage will be crisp and the flavor delicious.

Serve a small pitcher of vinegar on the side.

SERVES 4 TO 6

LAYERED VEGETABLES

2 medium-size baking potatoes,
   peeled
3 medium-size carrots, peeled
1 large green pepper, seeded
   and sliced (directions below)
1 large onion, peeled and halved
Salt (if allowed) or salt
   substitute, or omit

Freshly ground black pepper
⅔ cup evaporated skim milk
⅓ cup water
1 beef bouillon cube
   (low-sodium, if desired)

Preheat oven to 375° F.

With slicing disc in place, slice all the vegetables separately. If not assembling the casserole immediately, place potato slices in cold water, draining well before using.

To slice the green pepper, cut in half to fit feed tube, giving half slices, or slit the whole pepper down one side, roll up tightly, insert from bottom of feed tube (making sure pepper is flat on slicing disc), and slice, using medium pressure. This gives you slices that can be reshaped into rings.

Layer the vegetables in a 1½-quart casserole. Lightly salt (if using) and pepper the layers as you go.

Heat milk and water and dissolve bouillon cube. Pour over vegetables, cover, and bake about 45 minutes, or until vegetables are tender and liquid has been absorbed.

SERVES 4 TO 6

WINE-BRAISED CABBAGE

1 small head cabbage
4 scallions, with some green
   tops
4 tablespoons margarine
Freshly ground black pepper
Salt (if allowed) or salt
   substitute, or omit

½ cup dry vermouth or white
   wine (or more)
½ teaspoon caraway seeds, or
   to taste (optional)

With shredding disc in place, core and cut cabbage into pieces to fit feed tube. Shred cabbage and scallions, using medium pressure.

In heavy sauté or frying pan large enough to hold comfortably all the cabbage and scallions, melt margarine and add vegetables.

Add pepper and salt (if used) to taste and sauté over medium heat for about 10 minutes, or until cabbage is limp. Add wine, cover closely, and simmer gently for 30 to 35 minutes, checking occasionally to be sure cabbage is not drying out. There should be little or no liquid remaining at the end of the cooking time. Should cabbage appear to be drying out, however, add a tablespoon or more wine or water.

Serve sprinkled with caraway seeds, if desired.

SERVES ABOUT 4

BAKED TOMATOES AND . . .

This is a recipe that is wonderfully elastic. It all depends on what you have in the refrigerator and how many you need to serve. It is a delicious way to use leftover vegetables that aren't headed for the soup pot. The basic ingredients are:

*Nice-size tomatoes—1 for each
  2 being served
Cornflake, shredded wheat, or
  cracker crumbs
Onion or scallions, white part
  only
Vegetables—spinach, broccoli,
  asparagus, beans—anything
  that goes well with tomatoes*

*Low-fat creamed cottage cheese
Grated sapsago or Parmesan
  cheese
Salt (if allowed) or salt
  substitute, or omit
Additional herbs*

Preheat oven to 375° F.

Cut each tomato in half. Cut ends flat and place on oiled baking sheet large enough to hold however many you are making.

With the steel knife in place, make enough crumbs from the suggested ingredients above—for 4 servings, about ½ cup is just right. Set aside. With machine running, add small piece of onion or 2 or 3 scallions and mince fine. Now add the vegetable (about ½ to ⅔ cup for 4 servings), cottage cheese (about ½ cup for 4 servings), grated cheese (¼ teaspoon sapsago or ½ teaspoon Parmesan), and seasonings to taste. Oregano is delicious with broccoli, for instance. Turn machine on and off just to blend. Add crumbs and turn machine on and off to mix.

Pile mixture evenly on tomato halves. Sprinkle with additional cheese if desired and allowed. Bake for 15 to 20 minutes, or until tomatoes are slightly soft and mixture is browned.

Experiment!

QUANTITIES GIVEN SERVE 4

CAULIFLOWER PURÉE

1 large head cauliflower	Salt (if allowed) or salt
4 to 5 sprigs parsley	substitute, or omit
2 tablespoons margarine	Freshly ground black pepper
½ teaspoon thyme	Chopped parsley for garnish

Wash cauliflower. Remove outer stalk leaves unless they are fresh. Cut out core and separate into flowerets. Cook flowerets (and leaves, if fresh) in boiling water, covered, until tender—5 to 8 minutes. Drain well.

With steel knife in place, chop parsley, turning machine on and off until quite fine. Add remaining ingredients with cauliflower to work bowl. Purée mixture, turning machine on and off, then letting machine run until smooth.

Serve sprinkled with additional chopped parsley.

SERVES 4

PEPPERS AND SQUASH

---

4 small zucchini or a
   combination of zucchini and
   small yellow squash
4 small green peppers, seeded
1 large tomato
⅓ cup oil

Salt (if allowed) or salt
   substitute, or omit
Pinch of dried basil, or to taste
1 teaspoon sugar
Freshly ground black pepper

With steel knife in place, cut vegetables into chunks and chop coarsely, turning machine on and off. Use about 1½ cups vegetables for each batch.

Heat oil in heavy skillet and sauté chopped vegetables over medium heat for 10 minutes. Add remaining ingredients to taste, cover, and simmer for another 10 minutes.

SERVES 4 TO 6

CARROTS AND BEAN SPROUTS

1 small onion, peeled
3 large carrots, peeled
2 tablespoons oil
1 (1-pound) can bean sprouts,
  drained and rinsed

Chopped chives, poppy seeds,
  or celery seed to taste

With steel knife in place, quarter onion and chop coarsely.
Reserve.

With shredding disc in place, cut carrots into lengths to fit
crosswise in feed tube and shred.

Heat oil in heavy skillet and sauté onion and carrots over medium heat for 5 minutes. Add ¼ cup water, cover, and simmer
for another 5 minutes.

Mix in bean sprouts and cook, uncovered, over medium heat,
stirring, until heated through.

Serve with any of the suggested seasonings, or try your own.

SERVES 4 TO 6

DRUNKEN CARROTS

This is an expandable recipe. To suit the number of people you are serving, just add more carrots and adjust the rest of the ingredients accord-
ingly. Basically you need:

¼ cup parsley sprigs
1 pound carrots, peeled and cut
  into lengths to fit crosswise
  in feed tube

½ cup water
3 tablespoons margarine
2 or 3 tablespoons Cointreau,
  Cognac, or other brandy

With steel knife in place, add parsley and mince fine. Set aside.

With french fry disc in place, process the carrots into nicely curved sticks.

In heavy saucepan, add carrots to ½ cup boiling water and simmer, covered, about 8 to 10 minutes. They should be just tender. Drain, add margarine and Cointreau (or your choice), and over medium heat stir or shake gently until carrots are glazed.

Just before serving, mix in reserved minced parsley or sprinkle on top.

1 POUND CARROTS SERVES 3 TO 4

CRUSTY PARSNIPS

⅓ cup fresh bread crumbs
1 pound fresh parsnips
3 tablespoons margarine
Skim milk
¼ teaspoon ground cardamom

Salt (if allowed) or salt
    substitute, or omit
1 tablespoon sesame seeds
Additional margarine
    (optional)

Preheat oven to 400° F.

With steel knife in place, reduce enough good white bread, crusts removed, to make ⅓ cup crumbs. Set aside.

Cook parsnips in boiling water to cover until tender. Plunge immediately into cold water to make them easier to handle. Peel parsnips, cut into 1-inch pieces, and, with steel knife in place, purée the parsnips, turning machine on and off, then letting machine run until mixture is smooth. Add the 3 tablespoons margarine, some skim milk if mixture is too thick, cardamom, and salt (if used) to taste. Turn machine on and off to mix.

Turn into greased 1-quart casserole and sprinkle with reserved bread crumbs and the sesame seeds. If desired, dot with additional margarine.

Bake uncovered for 20 to 25 minutes, or until topping is slightly brown.

SERVES 3 TO 4

BAKED EGGPLANT

1 large eggplant, peeled and
   diced
½ cup shredded wheat or
   cornflake crumbs
2 cloves garlic, peeled
2 medium-size onions, peeled
   and quartered
3 tablespoons oil
2 medium-size tomatoes, peeled

1 tablespoon lemon juice
Salt (if allowed) or salt
   substitute, or omit
Freshly ground black pepper
Suggested additional seasonings:
   celery seed, oregano, thyme,
   marjoram, allspice—a pinch
   of any one
Cheese Crumbs (see index)

Preheat oven to 350° F.

Cook peeled and diced eggplant in boiling water, covered, for 10 minutes. Drain well and reserve.

With steel knife in place, reduce shredded wheat or cornflakes to crumbs and set aside.

With steel knife in place and with machine running, drop garlic through feed tube. Turn machine on and off to mince. Add quartered onions and turn machine on and off until well chopped.

Heat oil in heavy skillet and sauté garlic-onion mixture over medium heat until soft but not brown.

Quarter tomatoes and, with steel knife in place, chop coarsely, turning machine on and off. Add to onion mixture and cook an additional 10 minutes, stirring constantly. Add lemon juice, reserved crumbs, and seasonings to taste.

With steel knife in place, purée eggplant, turning machine on and off, then letting machine run until mixture is smooth. Combine eggplant with onion-tomato mixture. Turn into 1-quart casserole and sprinkle with Cheese Crumbs. Bake uncovered for 20 to 25 minutes.

SERVES 4 TO 6

SPECIAL TURNIPS

---

1 pound turnips, peeled and cut
   into lengths to fit crosswise in
   feed tube
1 small onion, peeled
1 cup chicken bouillon
   (low-sodium, if desired)

1 tablespoon margarine
1 teaspoon sugar (or substitute)
1 tablespoon chopped parsley
Freshly ground pepper
⅛ to ¼ teaspoon ground
   ginger (optional)

With french fry disc in place, process turnips and onion. Heat chicken bouillon in heavy saucepan and add vegetables. Bring to a boil and simmer, covered, about 20 minutes, or until tender. Drain well. Add margarine, sugar, parsley, and pepper to taste.

Variation: Add all the cooked ingredients, including some ginger if you like, to the food processor bowl with the steel knife in place. Purée mixture, turning machine on and off, then letting machine run until mixture is smooth. Serve sprinkled with additional parsley.

SERVES 3 TO 4

BRAISED CELERY HEARTS

Celery and carrots are two vegetables that have a higher salt content than most other vegetables. It is a fact to keep in mind if sodium restriction is particularly rigid.

1 celery heart
4 scallions, with some green
   parts
3 tablespoons oil or margarine
½ cup chicken or beef bouillon
   (low-sodium, if desired)
½ cup plain low-fat yogurt

Salt (if allowed) or salt
   substitute, or omit
Freshly ground black pepper
Grated Parmesan or sapsago
   cheese for garnish
Chopped parsley for garnish

With slicing disc in place, cut celery into lengths to fit feed tube and slice, using medium pressure. Slice scallions.

In heavy skillet, heat oil or margarine. Add celery and scallions and sauté over medium heat for a few minutes. Add bouillon, cover, and simmer until celery is tender-crisp, about 8 to 10 minutes.

Stir in yogurt and seasonings to taste. When ready to serve, turn into serving dish and sprinkle with cheese and parsley.

SERVES 4

NUTTY SQUASH

¼ cup coarsely chopped
   walnuts
1 small onion, peeled and
   quartered
4 medium-size zucchini or 2
   zucchini and 2 yellow squash
2 tablespoons oil or margarine

2 tablespoons water
1 tablespoon dry sherry—more
   if desired
Salt (if allowed) or salt
   substitute, or omit
Freshly ground black pepper

With steel knife in place, add walnuts and chop coarsely, turning machine on and off. Set aside.

Add quartered onion and chop coarsely, turning machine on and off. Set aside.

With slicing disc in place, cut zucchini to fit feed tube and slice. In heavy saucepan, heat oil or margarine and sauté onion and zucchini over low heat for about 5 minutes. Add water and sherry, cover, and cook 3 or 4 minutes more, or until just tender.

Add reserved walnuts and seasonings to taste and serve immediately.

SERVES 4

CURRIED SQUASH

2 medium-size yellow squash
2 medium-size zucchini
3 tablespoons margarine
¼ teaspoon curry powder, or
   to taste

Salt (if allowed) or salt
   substitute, or omit
Freshly ground black pepper
Chopped chives or parsley for
   garnish

Cut yellow squash and zucchini into lengths to fit feed tube and, with slicing disc in place, slice, using medium pressure.

Cook squash and zucchini in small amount of water, covered, until just tender—about 5 minutes. Drain thoroughly.

In small saucepan, melt margarine, stir in curry powder and salt (if used) and pepper to taste. Stir lightly into cooked squash. Serve squash sprinkled with chopped chives or parsley.

SERVES 4

ZUCCHINI AND ONIONS

3 to 4 medium-size zucchini
2 small onions, peeled
3 tablespoons oil
Garlic powder to taste
Salt (if allowed) or salt
   substitute to taste, or omit

Freshly ground black pepper to
   taste
Pinch of oregano (optional, but
   good)
Grated sapsago or Parmesan
   cheese

With slicing disc in place, slice zucchini and onions, using medium pressure.

Heat oil in heavy skillet and sauté vegetables slowly over low to medium heat, stirring, until tender—15 to 20 minutes. Add seasonings and serve sprinkled with grated cheese.

SERVES 4

PURÉED BRUSSELS SPROUTS

Brussels sprouts have never been a favorite vegetable at our house. However, with the food processor and some judicious seasoning, we find them quite acceptable.

4 cups Brussels sprouts
Salt (if allowed) or salt
  substitute to taste, or omit
1 teaspoon nutmeg

¼ cup plain low-fat yogurt
2 tablespoons dry sherry
  (optional, but nice)

Wash and trim Brussels sprouts. Just cover with water and simmer, covered, until tender. Drain.

With steel knife in place, purée Brussels sprouts in batches, turning machine on and off, then letting machine run until mixture is smooth. Return to saucepan and stir in seasonings, yogurt, and sherry. Reheat, but do not boil.

For a change of taste, try some oregano, marjoram, mustard, or thyme.

SERVES 4 TO 6

PURÉE OF PEAS AND WATER CHESTNUTS

This recipe is one example of how the food processor allows you to combine two foods of varying texture to make a delicious and interesting dish. The addition of the crunchy water chestnuts makes an otherwise plain vegetable memorable.

2 (10-ounce) packages frozen peas (the petite ones are delicious)
1 (8-ounce) can water chestnuts, drained

Salt (if allowed) or salt substitute, or omit
Freshly ground black pepper
Chopped fresh mint (optional)

Cook peas according to package directions and drain.

With steel knife in place, chop water chestnuts, turning machine on and off until well chopped but still retaining texture. Set aside in heavy saucepan.

Purée peas, turning machine on and off, then letting machine run until smooth. Add puréed peas to water chestnuts in saucepan, stir well to combine, and add salt (if used), pepper, and mint to taste. Reheat just before serving.

Variation: Substitute spinach for peas and season with 1 tablespoon low-fat yogurt and a dash of nutmeg.

SERVES 4 TO 6

MUSHROOMS STUFFED WITH PURÉE OF PEAS AND WATER CHESTNUTS

This is a tasty variation on the preceding recipe.

*Recipe for Purée of Peas and
    Water Chestnuts, omitting
    mint and adding ⅛ teaspoon
    thyme, ⅛ to ¼ teaspoon
    onion powder, or to taste,
    and 2 tablespoons melted
    margarine*

*14 large mushroom caps
¼ cup melted margarine
Cheese Crumbs (see index)*

Preheat oven to 400° F.

Prepare recipe for Purée of Peas and Water Chestnuts.

Remove stems from mushrooms and reserve for soup. Wipe mushroom caps and dip lightly in melted margarine. Place hollow side up in lightly greased baking dish. Fill caps with pea purée, sprinkle with Cheese Crumbs, and bake for 15 minutes, or until crumbs are browned and mixture is heated through. These stuffed mushrooms are attractive surrounding a platter of sliced meat.

DEPENDING ON APPETITES, PLAN ON EITHER 1 OR 2
MUSHROOMS PER PERSON

VEGETABLES VINAIGRETTE

Almost any vegetable, sliced, shredded, or french-cut in the food processor, cooked to a tender-crisp stage, then drained and marinated in the following basic vinaigrette dressing, singly or in combination, adds interest and variety to a meal.

Vinaigrette dressing is simply the classic French dressing (usually 3 parts oil to 1 part vinegar, but depending on personal preference and the flavor and strength of the oil and vinegar) with additional herbs.

½ clove garlic or 1 tablespoon
  minced onion
¾ cup oil
¼ cup vinegar
Salt (if allowed) or salt
  substitute to taste, or omit

Freshly ground black pepper to
  taste
1 teaspoon chopped chives,
  chervil, or parsley, or a
  mixture of all 3

With steel knife in place and with machine running, drop garlic or small piece of onion through feed tube. Turn machine on and off until finely minced. Add remaining ingredients, turning machine on and off to mix well. Refrigerate and shake well before mixing with vegetables.

MAKES 1 CUP

BRAISED RADISHES

Low-cholesterol, low-fat, and with the ease of slicing in the food processor, the recipe is a natural for this diet.

2 bunches radishes—about 2
  cups, sliced
2 tablespoons margarine
¼ cup chicken or beef bouillon
  (low-sodium, if desired)

Pinch of marjoram or thyme, or
  to taste

Clean radishes. With slicing disc in place, fill feed tube with radishes and slice. It doesn't matter how you fill the feed tube, the radishes always come out beautifully sliced.

Melt margarine in heavy skillet or saucepan. Add radishes and sauté for 5 minutes. Add bouillon and seasonings, cover, and simmer over medium heat for 5 minutes. Serve hot.

SERVES 4

ESCALLOPED POTATOES

1 medium-size onion, peeled
4 medium-size baking potatoes,
  peeled
Salt (if allowed) or salt
  substitute, or omit

Freshly ground black pepper
1¼ cups skim milk mixed with
  ½ cup dry skim milk, or 1¼
  cups evaporated skim milk
2 tablespoons oil or margarine

Preheat oven to 350° F.

With shredding disc in place, shred onion and set aside.

With slicing disc in place, slice potatoes.

In lightly oiled 1½-quart casserole, layer potatoes, onions, and salt (if used) and pepper to taste, ending with some shredded onion.

Heat milk and oil or margarine and pour over potatoes. The liquid should come just to the top without covering. Bake uncovered for 1¼ hours or until potatoes are tender and browned.

Variation: Instead of using all milk for liquid, use half beef or chicken bouillon (low-sodium, if desired) and half milk. Sprinkle the top with Parmesan or paprika before baking.

SERVES 4 TO 6

NOUILLES AUX FROMAGES

This is a delicious—and somewhat higher in calorie—change from potatoes or rice. Make certain the noodles are made from wheat and not enriched with egg yolks. You can also use macaroni, but then the name will have to be changed.

8 ounces noodles (or macaroni)
¼ cup parsley sprigs
6 scallions, white part only
½ clove garlic (optional)
8 ounces low-fat creamed cottage cheese
1 tablespoon bleu cheese
2 tablespoons oil

1 teaspoon butter flavoring
½ cup Fleischmann's Egg Beaters
Salt (if allowed) or salt substitute to taste, or omit
Freshly ground black pepper to taste

Preheat oven to 350° F.

Cook noodles according to package directions, omitting salt from cooking water if desired, drain, and set aside.

With steel knife in place, add parsley. Turn machine on and off until finely minced. With machine running, drop scallions and garlic through feed tube. Turn machine on and off to mince. Add remaining ingredients. Turn machine on and off, then let run for 20 seconds.

In large mixing bowl, combine reserved noodles and cheese mixture. Turn into 1½-quart casserole and bake uncovered for 35 to 40 minutes, or until mixture is set.

SERVES 4 TO 6

CRISPY OVEN FRIES

This is a simple recipe for potatoes whose quantity can be increased or decreased with ease. Done with the french fry disc, the rule of thumb is 1 medium-size potato for 2 moderate servings.

Baking potatoes, peeled and cut into pieces to fit crosswise in feed tube

Oil
Salt (if allowed) or salt substitute, or omit

Preheat oven to 400° F.

With the french fry disc in place, process as many potatoes as you are using, emptying the work bowl when full into a bowl of ice water to prevent discoloring.

Use a shallow baking pan large enough to arrange the potato sticks in a single layer. Pour just enough oil to cover the bottom of the pan, then add 1 more tablespoon.

Dry potatoes thoroughly between paper towels and distribute them evenly over the baking pan. With your hands, roll the potatoes in the oil until each piece is well coated.

Bake for 35 to 40 minutes until browned and crisp. Watch closely the last few minutes, since they burn quickly. Turn out onto paper towels and drain thoroughly. Sprinkle with salt (if used).

These make wonderful cocktail snacks—try sprinkling with low-sodium seasoned salt—as well as a tasty accompaniment to other meals.

SERVES AS MANY AS NEEDED, ALLOWING 1 MEDIUM-SIZE
POTATO FOR 2 SERVINGS

Main-Course Luncheon and Dinner Dishes

About Main-Course Luncheon and Dinner Dishes

One of the most difficult tasks for the cook is to use effectively the list of YES, NO, AND SOMETIMES food provided by the patient's physician and the hospital dietician and to maintain a tasteful and balanced day-by-day diet. This is especially important when family and/or guests are present.

The following recipes offer a wide variety of main-course luncheon and dinner dishes, well within the requirements of the low-cholesterol, low-sodium, low-fat diet. Many recipes that might otherwise be restricted are offered, using substitute ingredients but tasting and looking as good as the original.

With the food processor, all the recipes are easily prepared and the wide range of recipe selection will facilitate that day-to-day meal planning.

SALMON PUFFS FOR TWO

⅔ cup cornflakes
4 to 5 sprigs parsley
1 tablespoon dried minced
  onion
1 teaspoon dried dill weed
Freshly ground black pepper
Salt (if allowed) or salt
  substitute, or omit
1 tablespoon soft margarine

1 tablespoon lemon juice
½ cup skim milk
1 egg or ¼ cup Fleischmann's
  Egg Beaters
1 (7¾-ounce) can salmon,
  drained
Cucumber Sauce II (recipe
  follows)

Preheat oven to 350° F.

With steel knife in place, add cornflakes. Turn machine on and off, then let whirl until reduced to fine crumbs. Set aside.

Add parsley and turn machine on and off until minced. Return cornflake crumbs to bowl and add all ingredients except salmon and sauce. Turn machine on and off, then let run for 4 seconds, scraping down sides, if necessary. Add salmon and turn machine on and off, then let machine run for 4 seconds.

Divide mixture into 2 individual 5-inch ramekins. Place in baking dish filled with ½ inch water. Bake for 40 minutes. Serve with Cucumber Sauce II.

SERVES 2

CUCUMBER SAUCE II

1 small cucumber, peeled
1 tablespoon dried minced
  onion
¼ cup mayonnaise (see index)

2 teaspoons vinegar
¼ cup plain low-fat yogurt
Minced parsley or dried dill
  weed

With shredding disc in place, shred cucumber and set aside to drain well. With steel knife in place, add remaining ingredients and turn machine on and off to mix. Fold in cucumber. Refrigerate until served.

MAKES ⅔ CUP

FISH MIREPOIX

A *mirepoix* is a mixture of vegetables used in meat, fish, and shellfish dishes to heighten their flavor.

2 stalks celery, cut into 1-inch
  pieces
1 small onion, peeled and
  quartered

1 medium-size carrot, peeled
  and cut into 1-inch pieces
½ green pepper, seeded
3 tablespoons margarine or oil

1 pound flounder or other
white fish fillets, cut into
serving-size pieces
½ cup dry white wine

Paprika
Chopped parsley for garnish
Lemon wedges

With steel knife in place, chop vegetables, using on and off turns until coarsely chopped.

Heat margarine or oil in skillet large enough to hold fillets in one layer. Add vegetables and sauté over moderate heat about 10 minutes, stirring frequently. Lay fillets in single layer over vegetables. Pour wine over the fillets and sprinkle with paprika. Cover skillet and cook over heat just hot enough to let the vegetables bubble slowly—about 10 minutes or until fish flakes easily.

Serve fish with the mirepoix and sprinkle with chopped parsley. Pass lemon wedges.

SERVES 3 TO 4

FISH FILLETS IN HERB-WINE SAUCE

1½ pounds flounder fillets, or
other white fish, cut into
serving-size pieces
⅓ cup parsley sprigs
½ clove garlic, peeled
3 scallions, white part only

½ teaspoon tarragon
2 tablespoons melted margarine
2 tablespoons flour
½ cup dry white wine
¼ cup evaporated skim milk
Chopped parsley for garnish

Preheat oven to 350° F.

Arrange fillets in single layer in greased baking dish.

With steel knife in place, add parsley sprigs. Turn machine on and off until minced. With machine running, drop garlic and scallions through feed tube. Turn machine on and off until minced. Add remaining ingredients, except parsley for garnish. Turn machine on and off, then let run for 5 seconds. Pour wine sauce over fillets. Bake uncovered for 30 minutes, or until fish flakes easily.

Serve sprinkled with chopped parsley.

SERVES 4 TO 6

OVEN-GOING ROLLED FISH FILLETS

1 small lemon
1 medium-size onion, peeled
¼ pound mushrooms
1 tablespoon oil or margarine
¼ cup oil
½ cup tomato or cocktail vegetable juice (low-sodium, if desired)

1 tablespoon lemon juice
1 pound fish fillets
Garlic powder
Paprika
Chopped parsley for garnish
Lemon wedges

Preheat oven to 375° F.

Cut ends flat on lemon. With slicing disc in place, insert in feed tube and slice, using medium pressure. If lemon is too large to fit through top, turn cover over and insert from bottom. Set aside.

Cut onion to fit feed tube and slice. Set aside. Slice mushrooms. In heavy skillet, melt the 1 tablespoon oil or margarine and sauté onions and mushrooms over medium heat about 10 minutes. Spread on bottom of shallow oven-proof dish, large enough to hold fillets.

In mixing bowl, combine the ¼ cup oil and the tomato or cocktail vegetable juice and lemon juice. Dip each fillet in mixture, roll tightly, and place on vegetables. Pour remaining tomato mixture over fillets. Sprinkle with garlic powder and paprika. Place reserved lemon slices over fillets. Bake, uncovered, for 25 to 30 minutes, or until fish flakes easily.

Sprinkle with chopped parsley and serve with lemon wedges.

Variations: Stuff the fillets with Cheese Crumbs (see index) moistened with dry white wine or skim milk. Add your favorite herbs to the Cheese Crumbs mixture.

Or, in place of the sliced onion and mushroom base, utilize the processor to chop leftover vegetables, then surround the fillets with sliced mushrooms and cover with a mixture of mayonnaise, yogurt, and lemon juice. Add a pinch of tarragon and sprinkle with chopped parsley.

Experiment!

SERVES 3 TO 4

SESAME BAKED HADDOCK

Although the food processor is utilized for the bread crumbs only, and the amount of margarine (fat) is high, this is delicious if the calories can be tolerated.

2 tablespoons toasted sesame seeds

2 cups soft bread crumbs (about 5 slices French or low-sodium bread)

1 pound haddock fillets, cut into serving-size pieces

Salt (if allowed) or salt substitute, or omit

Freshly ground black pepper

Margarine, cut into ¼-inch slices

¼ teaspoon thyme

¼ cup melted margarine

Lemon wedges

Preheat oven to 350° F.

To toast sesame seeds, place sesame seeds in pie plate and bake until lightly browned. Set aside.

With steel knife in place, tear bread into pieces and add to work bowl. Turn machine on and off, then let machine run until reduced to crumbs. Set aside.

Place fish pieces close together in oiled baking dish. Sprinkle with salt (if used) and pepper to taste. Top each piece with a slice of margarine.

Combine reserved sesame seeds and bread crumbs, thyme, and the ¼ cup melted margarine. Arrange over fish, covering completely.

Bake uncovered for 25 to 30 minutes, or until crumb topping is lightly browned.

Serve with lemon wedges.

SERVES 3 TO 4

EASY, EASY BAKED FISH

1 pound fresh or frozen white fish, cut into serving-size pieces
1 cup skim milk
Salt (if allowed) or salt substitute, or omit
½ cup cornflake or shredded wheat crumbs

¼ cup parsley sprigs
1 large onion, peeled
1 tablespoon lemon juice (or dry white wine) combined with ½ cup plain low-fat yogurt

Preheat oven to 400° F.

Soak fish in salted (if allowed) skim milk for 1 hour.

With steel knife in place, reduce enough cornflakes or shredded wheat to make ½ cup crumbs. Set aside.

Chop parsley, turning machine on and off. Set aside.

With shredding disc in place, cut onion to fit feed tube and shred, using medium pressure. Set aside.

Without drying fish, remove from milk and dip in crumbs. Place pieces close together in lightly greased baking dish. Sprinkle with reserved grated onion and chopped parsley.

Mix lemon juice or wine and yogurt and spread over fillets. Bake uncovered for 20 minutes, or until fish flakes easily.

SERVES 3 TO 4

FISH FLORENTINE NEWBURG

1 medium-size onion, peeled
1 (8-ounce) bottle clam juice
4 parsley sprigs
½ cup celery leaves
1 bay leaf
½ cup dry white wine
2 pounds white fish or fresh salmon, cut into serving-size pieces

2 (10-ounce) packages frozen chopped spinach
1 cup plain low-fat yogurt
1 tablespoon lemon juice
Mock Newburg Sauce (recipe follows)
1 tablespoon grated Parmesan cheese

Preheat oven to 450° F.

With slicing disc in place, cut onion to fit feed tube and slice, using medium pressure. Add onion to heavy skillet with clam juice, parsley, celery, bay leaf, and wine. Bring to a boil. Add fish and simmer gently for 5 to 8 minutes—no longer than it takes to have fish flake easily. Carefully lift out fish with slotted spatula and set aside.

Cook spinach according to package directions. Drain *thoroughly*, discarding liquid. Mix spinach with yogurt and lemon juice.

Divide spinach mixture into 6 or 8 individual shells or 1 large, lightly oiled baking pan. Divide fish between shells or arrange in large pan. Cover with Mock Newburg Sauce and sprinkle with Parmesan cheese. Place in oven just long enough to heat through.

MOCK NEWBURG SAUCE

This Newburg Sauce is not the classic combination of heavy cream thickened with egg yolks, served originally at the famous Delmonico's restaurant, but it is delicious and deserves a place in this diet.

⅓ cup parsley sprigs	Salt (if allowed) or salt
½ cup plain low-fat yogurt	substitute to taste, or omit
½ cup mayonnaise (see index)	White pepper to taste
¼ cup dry sherry	Grated nutmeg to taste

With steel knife in place, add parsley. Turn machine on and off to mince. Add remaining ingredients. Turn machine on and off to mix well.

This sauce can be used in other recipes calling for a Newburg Sauce. Heat in double boiler and serve over any baked fish fillets.

SERVES 6 TO 8

SWEDISH FISH PUDDING

This recipe is a legacy from my Swedish grandmother. With the aid of the food processor in grinding the fish and a few changes in the original rich ingredients, it is a quick and delicious luncheon or supper dish.

1 pound lean white fish, cut into chunks
1 tablespoon margarine
1 tablespoon cornstarch
1 cup evaporated skim milk
1 whole egg or 2 egg whites or ¼ cup Fleischmann's Egg Beaters

Salt (if allowed) or salt substitute, or omit
White pepper
Grated nutmeg to taste
1 tablespoon cornflake or cracker crumbs
Tangy Dill Sauce (recipe follows)

Preheat oven to 350° F.

With steel knife in place, add fish to work bowl. Turn machine on and off several times, then let machine run for 5 seconds. Add remaining ingredients except crumbs and sauce. Turn machine on and off, then let machine run for 10 seconds, or until fish is completely puréed and mixture is very smooth.

Lightly oil a 1-quart ring or other mold and sprinkle with crumbs. Turn fish mixture into mold. Set mold in pan of hot water—about 1 inch in depth—and bake uncovered for 1 hour, or until a silver knife inserted in the center comes out clean, indicating the pudding is set all the way through. Serve, unmolded, either hot or cold with Tangy Dill Sauce.

TANGY DILL SAUCE

2 tablespoons or more fresh dill
  or 1½ teaspoons dried dill
  weed
3 scallions, white part only
2 tablespoons sugar (or
  substitute)
1 tablespoon lemon juice

1 cup good wine vinegar
Dash of cayenne
Dash of hot pepper sauce
  (optional)
1 teaspoon powdered mustard,
  or to taste

With steel knife in place, add dill and scallions. Turn machine on and off to chop. Add remaining ingredients. Turn machine on and off until scallions are finely chopped and ingredients well mixed. Chill thoroughly and shake well before using. Serve with Swedish Fish Pudding.

MAKES ABOUT 1 CUP SAUCE

Variation: Substitute fresh salmon for white fish. Instead of the Tangy Dill Sauce, try mixing some shredded, drained cucumber and dried dill weed with your own mayonnaise. Or add low-sodium catsup or chili sauce and grated onion to the mayonnaise.

SERVES 4 TO 6

Chopped Meats

The first meat grinder is attributed to the chef to King Louis IX, who invented a little wheel with cutting edges and a small tunnel through which one pushed food. Refinements on that first meat grinder have kept the world in preground meats ever since.

With the arrival on the culinary scene in 1973 of the Cuisinart food processor for home cooks, preground meats from the store became obsolete. Chopped meat for meat loaves, casseroles, hamburgers, and other recipes can now be as lean and fat-free as possible. Buy your own meat, trim off all visible fat, and chop to desired consistency in seconds.

These leaner chopped meats may be a bit dry when cooked, so in preparing them for pan-broiling, regular broiling, or baking, always add additional oil or other moisture. In pan-broiling, oil the pan lightly to keep the meat from sticking.

CHOPPED MEAT (not hamburgers) WITH A DIFFERENCE

Try the following additions to 1 pound of lean beef, trimmed, cut into 1-inch cubes, and chopped to desired consistency in your food processor.

※1

¼ cup finely chopped fresh
    mushrooms
¼ teaspoon marjoram or thyme
1 tablespoon oil

¼ cup dry white wine
Salt (if allowed) or salt
    substitute, or omit
Freshly ground black pepper

※2

6 to 8 water chestnuts, finely
    chopped
2 scallions, white part only,
    minced
¼ teaspoon oregano or Italian
    seasoning

1 tablespoon oil
1 tablespoon low-sodium
    Worcestershire sauce

※3

1 small carrot, peeled and
    minced
3 scallions, white part only,
    minced

2 tablespoons minced green
    pepper
1 tablespoon oil
2 tablespoons dry red wine

With each of these recipes, with steel knife in place, chop meat, using on and off turns until desired consistency is reached. Set aside in mixing bowl.

Chop vegetables to desired consistency and add to meat with seasonings. Mix well with hands and let mixture sit at room temperature for at least 30 minutes to mingle flavors.

Lightly shape meat into 4 patties and cook as desired, being certain not to overcook.

Variations: Use part veal with the beef, or substitute lamb for beef. The choices are endless for the imaginative cook.

SERVES 4

BURGERS BOURGUIGNON

An elegant way to dress up chopped meat. Delicious done on the outdoor grill.

½ cup cornflake or unsalted
   cracker crumbs
2 scallions, with some green
   parts
1½ pounds lean beef, trimmed
   and cut into 1-inch pieces
1 egg white
1 tablespoon oil

2 tablespoons red Burgundy
   wine
Salt (if allowed) or salt
   substitute to taste, or omit
Freshly ground black pepper to
   taste
Basting Sauce (recipe follows)

With steel knife in place, reduce enough cornflakes or crackers to make ½ cup crumbs. Set aside in mixing bowl.

With machine running, drop scallions through feed tube. Turn machine on and off to chop. Add to mixing bowl with crumbs.

Chop meat in 2 batches, turning machine on and off until desired consistency is reached. When processing second batch, add remaining ingredients, except sauce. Add everything to mixing bowl and combine lightly with hands. Let mixture sit for at least 30 minutes at room temperature to mingle flavors. Shape into 6 patties and cook as desired, basting with the following mixture:

BASTING SAUCE

2 scallions, with some green
  parts

¼ cup margarine
¼ cup red Burgundy wine

With steel knife in place and with machine running, drop scallions through feed tube. Turn machine on and off until finely chopped. Melt margarine in saucepan and sauté scallions briefly over medium heat. Add Burgundy and keep sauce warm over low heat.

As patties are broiling, turn several times and baste with sauce.

SERVES 6

BARBECUED SLOPPY JOES

1½ pounds lean beef, trimmed
  and cut into 1-inch pieces
1 small green pepper, seeded
1 small onion, peeled and
  quartered
2 tablespoons oil
⅔ cup chili sauce (low-sodium,
  if desired)

⅓ cup catsup (low-sodium, if
  desired)
1 teaspoon prepared mustard
  (low-sodium, if desired)
1 teaspoon vinegar
1 teaspoon sugar (or substitute)
Toasted English muffin halves
  or rolls

With steel knife in place, chop meat in 2 batches, turning machine on and off until desired consistency is reached. Set aside.

Chop green pepper and onion, turning machine on and off until coarsely chopped.

Heat oil in heavy skillet and add meat and vegetables. Sauté mixture over medium heat until meat loses red color and vegetables are slightly limp. Add remaining ingredients and simmer, uncovered, for 20 to 30 minutes.

Serve spooned over toasted English muffin halves or other toasted rolls. Also delicious served over plain rice.

SERVES 6

MEAT AND CARROT MOUSSAKA

There is some disagreement about the origin of Moussaka. One reliable source attributes it to Romania, and others to Greece. It doesn't matter at this time, since this dish of certain unvarying characteristics but varied ingredients is delicious made in any country by any good, venturesome cook. You can find recipes for Moussaka—generally made from chopped meat and eggplant—that contain neither ingredient yet retain the original characteristics: topped with Béchamel Sauce and sprinkled with cheese and/or bread crumbs.

The following recipe is delicious with either lamb or beef—each gives the dish a different flavor.

CARROT LAYER

1 tablespoon (or to taste)
chopped fresh mint or
2 teaspoons (or to taste)
crumbled dry mint
¼ cup fine bread or cracker
crumbs
1 pound carrots, peeled

1 small onion, peeled
1 teaspoon sugar (or substitute)
¼ cup skim milk
Salt (if allowed) or salt
substitute, or omit
Freshly ground pepper

MEAT LAYER

1 pound lean lamb or beef,
trimmed and cut into 1-inch
pieces
1 tablespoon minced onion or
1 medium-size scallion, white
part only
1 tablespoon minced green
pepper

2 tablespoons oil or margarine
Salt (if allowed) or salt
substitute, or omit
Freshly ground black pepper
Allowable Béchamel Sauce
(recipe follows)
Additional margarine
(optional)

Preheat oven to 400° F.

With steel knife in place, chop fresh mint and set aside.

Reduce enough dry bread or crackers to make ¼ cup fine crumbs and set aside.

With slicing disc in place, cut carrots in lengths to fit feed tube and slice. Empty into large saucepan. Cut onion to fit feed tube and slice. Add to carrots in pan. Add enough water to barely cover vegetables. Bring to a boil and simmer, covered, until tender—about 10 minutes. Drain thoroughly.

With steel knife in place, purée carrot and onion mixture, adding sugar (or substitute), the reserved mint, and the milk. The mixture should be fairly moist. Season to taste with salt (if used) and pepper and place in bottom of shallow 2-quart baking dish.

For the meat layer, with steel knife in place, chop meat in 2 batches, turning machine on and off until desired consistency is reached. Add onion or scallion and green pepper to second batch while processing.

Melt the 2 tablespoons oil or margarine in heavy skillet and sauté meat and onion over medium heat, stirring to keep meat broken up. Cook until meat loses red color. Season to taste and spread over carrot mixture.

ALLOWABLE BÉCHAMEL SAUCE

2 scallions, white part only
1 tablespoon margarine
1 tablespoon flour
⅓ cup chicken bouillon
  (low-sodium, if desired)

2 tablespoons dry skim milk
⅓ cup plain low-fat yogurt
Salt (if allowed) or salt
  substitute, or omit
Freshly ground pepper

With steel knife in place and machine running, drop scallions through feed tube. Turn machine on and off until finely minced.

Melt margarine in heavy saucepan and sauté scallions over medium heat, stirring constantly, for 3 or 4 minutes. Add flour and mix well. Combine chicken bouillon with dry skim milk and add to pan, stirring rapidly over medium heat until thickened. Add yogurt, and salt (if used) and pepper to taste.

Cover meat mixture with Allowable Béchamel Sauce, sprinkle with reserved crumbs, and, if desired, dot with additional margarine. Bake, uncovered, for 15 to 20 minutes, or until crumbs are browned.

SERVES 4 TO 6

MACARONI AND BEEF

This is an expandable recipe. To serve 4, use:

1 cup raw macaroni—2 cups
  cooked
1 pound lean beef, trimmed, cut
  into 1-inch pieces

1 medium-size green pepper,
  seeded and quartered
1 small onion, peeled and
  quartered

½ pound fresh mushrooms or
    1 (8-ounce) can sliced
    mushrooms, drained
2 tablespoons oil
1 (1-pound) can stewed
    tomatoes (low-sodium, if
    desired), undrained
Salt (if allowed) or salt
    substitute, or omit

Freshly ground black pepper
Garlic powder
½ teaspoon Italian seasoning
2 teaspoons cornstarch, mixed
    with 2 tablespoons dry red
    wine (or cold water)
Parmesan cheese (optional)

Preheat oven to 350° F.

Cook macaroni according to package directions, omitting salt from cooking water if desired. Drain and set aside.

With steel knife in place, chop beef in 2 batches, turning machine on and off until desired consistency is reached. Set aside.

Chop green pepper and onion, turning machine on and off until coarsely chopped. Set aside.

With slicing disc in place, slice mushrooms.

In heavy skillet, heat oil and add meat, green pepper, onion, and mushrooms. Sauté over medium heat, stirring constantly, until meat is no longer pink. Add tomatoes with their liquid (break up tomatoes with spoon) and seasonings to taste. Bring to a boil, cover, and simmer for 15 to 20 minutes.

Mix cornstarch with wine and add to meat mixture, stirring until thickened. Fold in cooked macaroni. Place in 1½-quart casserole and sprinkle with Parmesan cheese, if desired. Bake uncovered for 15 to 20 minutes, or until bubbly.

SERVES 4—RECIPE CAN EASILY BE DOUBLED

ADJUSTABLE BEEF AND RICE

An expandable recipe, depending on how many people you wish to serve. For 4 to 6 servings, use:

1½ pounds lean beef, trimmed and cut into 1-inch pieces
2 tablespoons margarine
1 (1-pound) can stewed tomatoes with green pepper and onions, undrained

Onion and garlic powder
Freshly ground black pepper
¾ cup raw instant rice
Parmesan cheese

With steel knife in place, chop meat in 2 batches, turning machine on and off until desired consistency is reached. In large skillet, melt margarine and sauté beef over medium heat until no longer pink. Add tomatoes, undrained and broken up with spoon, and seasonings to taste. Bring to a boil, cover, and simmer for 35 to 40 minutes. Stir in rice, cover, and let stand 10 minutes.

Turn into serving dish and sprinkle with Parmesan cheese, if desired.

Variations: Add a pinch of basil or oregano or Italian seasoning. For a low-sodium diet, use low-sodium stewed tomatoes, chop ½ green pepper and 4 scallions with beef, and sauté with beef. Omit onion powder and add ¼ teaspoon sugar substitute.

Also use mixture to stuff precooked whole green peppers. Preheat oven to 350° F. Place filled peppers on baking sheet. Pour low-sodium chili sauce or catsup over the tops and sprinkle with Parmesan cheese. Bake for 25 to 30 minutes.

SERVES 4 TO 6

CHILI CON CARNE

1 pound lean beef, trimmed and cut into 1-inch pieces

1 medium-size onion, peeled and quartered

1 medium-size green pepper, seeded and quartered

2 tablespoons oil

1 (1-pound) can tomatoes (low-sodium, if desired), undrained

1 tablespoon chili powder (or to taste)

Salt (if allowed) or salt substitute to taste, or omit

Freshly ground black pepper to taste

Garlic powder to taste

1 (1-pound) can kidney beans with liquid

Plain boiled rice (optional)

With steel knife in place, chop meat in 2 batches, turning machine on and off until desired consistency is reached. Set aside.

Chop onion and green pepper, turning machine on and off until coarsely chopped.

Heat oil in heavy skillet and add beef and vegetables. Sauté mixture over medium heat, stirring occasionally, until meat is no longer pink and vegetables are limp.

Add tomatoes, undrained and broken up with spoon, and remaining ingredients. Simmer, uncovered, over low heat, for about 1 hour, stirring occasionally.

This is delicious served on plain boiled rice—add a green salad and dinner is ready.

SERVES 4 TO 6

STUFFED EGGPLANT

This is an expandable recipe. To serve 4, use:

2 medium-size eggplants, washed and split lengthwise

1 pound lean beef, trimmed and cut into 1-inch pieces

2 small onions, peeled and quartered

1 small green pepper, seeded and quartered

2 tablespoons oil

½ cup tomato sauce or catsup (low-sodium, if desired)

½ teaspoon oregano or Italian seasoning

Salt (if allowed) or salt substitute, or omit

Freshly ground black pepper

2 tablespoons dry red wine

Grated Parmesan cheese

1 tablespoon oil

Preheat oven to 350° F.

Scoop pulp out of eggplant halves, leaving about ⅛-inch shell. With steel knife in place, drop eggplant pulp into work bowl and chunk, turning machine on and off. Set aside.

Chop beef in 2 batches, turning machine on and off until desired consistency is reached. Set aside. Chop onions and green pepper, turning machine on and off until coarsely chopped.

Heat the 2 tablespoons oil in heavy skillet and sauté onions and pepper over medium heat for 5 minutes. Add beef and sauté until it is no longer pink. Add reserved eggplant pulp, tomato sauce, seasonings to taste, and wine. Cover and simmer gently for 10 minutes.

Place eggplant shells on oiled baking sheet. Fill with meat mixture, sprinkle with Parmesan, and drizzle the 1 tablespoon oil over. Bake for about 35 to 40 minutes.

Variation: Use lean lamb instead of beef. Substitute garlic powder and rosemary for the oregano or Italian seasoning. Instead of sprinkling with Parmesan cheese, place a sliced tomato on top of each stuffed eggplant half, sprinkle with chopped parsley, then drizzle oil over.

SERVES 4

MEAT-"CRUST" PIZZA

Use chopped meat for the crust. Garnish with a variety of sliced vegetables and herbs. All the mozzarella cheese has been eliminated, but with a sprinkle of Parmesan, you almost won't notice!

½ cup cornflake crumbs
½ clove garlic peeled
(optional)
1 pound lean beef, trimmed and
cut into 1-inch pieces

¼ cup evaporated skim milk
1 tablespoon oil

With steel knife in place, reduce enough cornflakes to make ½ cup crumbs. Set aside in mixing bowl. Mince garlic, if used.

Add beef to garlic in work bowl in 2 batches, turning machine on and off until desired consistency is obtained. Add to mixing bowl with crumbs. Add milk and oil and mix well with hands. Pat into a 9-inch pie plate, raising rim about ½ inch around edge.

FILLING

⅓ cup tomato sauce or catsup
  (low-sodium, if desired)
Sliced mushrooms
Sliced onions or scallions, white
  part only
Sliced seeded green peppers
Sliced black olives (if allowed)

Sliced zucchini
Sliced tomatoes
Oil
Oregano or Italian seasoning, or
  your choice
Freshly ground black pepper
Parmesan cheese

Preheat oven to 400° F.

Spread tomato sauce or catsup over the meat "crust." With slicing disc in place, slice your choice of vegetables. Because the "crust" bakes in about 20 minutes, it is a good idea to sauté your choice of vegetables for a few minutes in oil before arranging them on the "crust."

Sprinkle with seasonings to taste and Parmesan cheese and bake for about 20 minutes.

Variation: For the "crust," use half beef and half veal. Or use half beef and half Simple Sausage Meat (see index). Experiment with other seasonings.

SERVES 4 TO 6

HERBED MEAT LOAF

1½ large shredded wheat
  biscuits
1½ pounds lean beef, trimmed
  and cut into 1-inch pieces
¼ cup minced onion (½
  medium-size onion)
¼ cup Fleischmann's Egg

Beaters or 1 egg white
½ teaspoon Italian seasoning
1 tablespoon oil
¼ cup skim milk
¼ cup dry red wine
Freshly ground black pepper to
  taste

Preheat oven to 350° F.

With steel knife in place, crumble shredded wheat biscuits into work bowl. Turn machine on and off, then let machine run until shredded wheat is reduced to fine crumbs. Set aside in large bowl.

Chop beef in 2 batches, turning machine on and off until desired consistency is obtained. Add to crumbs in mixing bowl.

Process onion, turning machine on and off until finely minced but not puréed. Add to meat mixture with remaining ingredients. Mix thoroughly with hands and pack lightly into a 9"×5"×3" loaf pan. Bake uncovered for 1 hour.

Variation: Add 1 tablespoon crumbled bleu cheese (if allowed) or 1 tablespoon grated sapsago cheese. Experiment with seasonings. For a variation in texture, coarsely chop 6 to 8 water chestnuts and add to meat mixture.

SERVES 6 OR MORE

HEARTY MEAT LOAF

1¼ pounds lean beef, trimmed
    and cut into 1-inch pieces
½ pound Simple Sausage Meat
    (see index)
2 medium-size potatoes,
    peeled and quartered
1 medium-size onion, peeled
    and quartered
1 small apple, peeled, seeded,
    and quartered

1 small green pepper, seeded
    and quartered
Salt (if allowed) or salt
    substitute, or omit
Freshly ground black pepper
⅔ cup evaporated skim milk
Pimiento strips (optional) for
    garnish

Preheat oven to 350° F.

With steel knife in place, chop the beef in 2 batches, turning machine on and off until meat is desired consistency. Place in large mixing bowl with Simple Sausage Meat.

Process potatoes, onion, apple, and green pepper in batches, turning machine on and off until coarsely chopped. Add to meat. Add seasonings to taste and skim milk and mix thoroughly with hands. Pack lightly in 9″×5″×3″ loaf pan. Garnish with pimiento strips, if desired. Cover with buttered foil and bake for 1 hour. Remove foil and bake 30 minutes longer.

This makes delicious sandwiches cold.

SERVES 6 TO 8

SPINACH-LAMB LOAF

1 (10-ounce) package frozen chopped spinach

½ cup cornflake, shredded wheat, or unsalted cracker crumbs

1½ pounds lean lamb, trimmed and cut into 1-inch pieces

½ clove garlic, peeled

4 scallions, white part only

¼ cup catsup (low-sodium if desired) or 1 small tomato, peeled

¼ cup skim milk or buttermilk

¼ cup Fleischmann's Egg Beaters or 1 egg white

½ teaspoon rosemary, crumbled (or to taste)

Salt (if allowed) or salt substitute to taste, or omit

Freshly ground black pepper to taste

Preheat oven to 350° F.

Defrost and drain spinach well. Set aside.

With steel knife in place, reduce enough cornflakes or other to make ½ cup fine crumbs. Set aside in large mixing bowl.

Chop lamb in 2 batches, turning machine on and off until desired consistency is reached. Add to cornflake crumbs in bowl. With machine running, drop garlic and scallions through feed tube. Turn machine on and off to mince. Add to meat.

If using small tomato, plunge into boiling water, then remove skin. With steel knife in place, turn machine on and off to chop fine. Add tomato or catsup to meat mixture with remaining ingredients, including spinach. Mix well with hands. Pack lightly into 9"×5"×3" loaf pan and bake uncovered for 1 hour.

Variation: Substitute beef for lamb and adjust seasonings. Omit rosemary and substitute thyme, oregano, or Italian seasoning.

SERVES 4 TO 6

LAMB EN PAPILLOTE

1 pound lean lamb, trimmed
and cut into 1-inch pieces
(lamb steak is suggested for
this recipe)
¼ cup parsley sprigs
1 small lemon

8 scallions, white part only
2 medium-size potatoes, peeled
1 medium-size zucchini
½ teaspoon garlic powder
½ teaspoon oregano
½ teaspoon rosemary

Preheat oven to 450° F.

Have ready 4 large squares of double thickness of aluminum foil. Divide the lamb evenly among the 4 squares.

With steel knife in place, chop parsley, turning machine on and off until minced. Set aside.

With slicing disc in place, cut both ends flat on lemon. Insert cut side down in feed tube. If too large to go through top, turn cover over and insert gently through bottom. Slice, using medium pressure. Set aside.

Slice scallions, potatoes, and zucchini separately and divide each among the 4 squares of foil with the meat. Sprinkle each portion with seasonings and reserved parsley and top with lemon slices. Carefully fold foil over and seal packets tightly. Place in shallow pan and bake for 1 hour.

You can vary the seasonings and vegetables and add freshly ground pepper.

SERVES 4

BAKED LAMBURGERS

¼ cup parsley sprigs
½ medium-size onion, peeled
1 pound lean lamb, trimmed
    and cut into 1-inch pieces
¼ teaspoon garlic powder (or
    to taste)

Salt (if allowed) or salt
    substitute, or omit
Freshly ground black pepper
Catsup or chili sauce
    (low-sodium, if desired)

Preheat oven to 350° F.

With steel knife in place, chop parsley, turning machine on and off. Set aside. Cut onion in half and chop, turning machine on and off until well chopped. Set aside in mixing bowl.

Chop lamb in 2 batches, turning machine on and off until desired consistency is reached. Add to onion with reserved parsley and seasonings to taste. Mix well with hands and form into 3 or 4 patties. Place in lightly oiled baking dish and cover each patty with 1 tablespoon catsup or chili sauce. Bake uncovered for 30 minutes.

Variation: Vary the seasonings. Try ½ to 1 teaspoon dried mint or marjoram or thyme or lemon rind. Add the catsup or chili sauce to the meat mixture and broil or pan-broil.

SERVES 3 TO 4

SIMPLE SAUSAGE MEAT

Not wishing to give up our weekend breakfast sausage, which was not allowable because of the high proportion of fat and off-limit seasonings in most commercial brands, I found the following recipe was the answer. In addition to its use in sautéed patties, it can be substituted for commercial sausage when this is called for in other recipes.

1½ pounds pork tenderloin	*Salt (if allowed) or salt*
1½ teaspoons poultry seasoning	*substitute to taste, or omit*
1 teaspoon sage	*Freshly ground black pepper to*
2 tablespoons oil	*taste*

Trim all visible fat from tenderloin. Cut into 1-inch cubes. With steel knife in place, process half the meat and half the other ingredients at a time, turning machine on and off until desired consistency is obtained. Mix batches together in large bowl, cover, and refrigerate overnight. Shape into patties to sauté or freeze for later use.

Brush skillet with oil. Start patties in cold skillet and sauté slowly over medium heat, turning frequently until browned. Because this sausage is lean, you may need a little more oil to keep the patties from sticking.

The amount of seasoning can be varied to suit.

SERVES 4 TO 6

BEEF BIRDS OR . . .

Roulades, paupiettes, rolladens, rollini, rollatine—by whatever name, they are delicious.

8 to 10 thin slices top round of beef, 1/8 inch thick and about 4 1/4 by 10 inches
1/2 cup cornflake or shredded wheat crumbs
1 tablespoon chopped parsley
1/4 pound fresh mushrooms
1 tablespoon freeze-dried chopped chives or onions
1 cup low-fat creamed cottage cheese
2 teaspoons grated sapsago or Parmesan cheese

1/4 teaspoon garlic powder
Salt (if allowed) or salt substitute, or omit
Freshly ground black pepper
Skim milk (optional)
4 tablespoons margarine or oil
1 cup or more dry red wine
1 cup or more beef bouillon (low-sodium, if desired)
1 tablespoon cornstarch (optional)
2 tablespoons dry red wine or cold water (optional)

Trim beef of all visible fat and set aside.

With steel knife in place, reduce enough cornflakes or shredded wheat to make 1/2 cup fine crumbs. Set aside.

Add several sprigs of parsley and chop, turning machine on and off, to make 1 tablespoon chopped. Add mushrooms and turn machine on and off until finely chopped. Add chives or onions, cheeses, garlic powder, salt (if used) and pepper to taste, and re-served crumbs. Turn machine on and off to mix well. If stuffing does not seem moist enough, add some skim milk.

Allow about 1 heaping tablespoon filling for each piece of beef. Place stuffing on one end and roll up, tucking in sides. Tie each beef roll with string.

Melt margarine in heavy skillet just large enough to hold the beef rolls in one layer. Brown beef lightly on all sides over me-dium heat. Add the 1 cup wine and the bouillon—enough to half cover the birds. Simmer, covered, for 1 hour, turning once or twice. Remove string before serving. If you wish to thicken the cooking liquid, mix 1 tablespoon cornstarch with 2 tablespoons dry red wine or cold water and add to liquid, stirring until thickened. Serve with birds.

Variation: Add ¼ teaspoon oregano or thyme or marjoram to stuffing mix. Simmer in the following sauce:

2 stalks celery

1 tomato, quartered

4 scallions, white part only

2 tablespoons flour

Salt (if allowed) or salt
  substitute to taste, or omit

Freshly ground black pepper to
  taste

¾ cup dry red wine

½ cup water (about)

With steel knife in place, chop celery with on and off turns. Add tomato and scallions and turn machine on and off to chop. Add remaining ingredients and turn machine on and off to mix thor-oughly. Pour over browned birds, adding wine and enough water to cover halfway. Finish cooking as above.

SERVES 6 TO 8

VEGETABLE-STUFFED FLANK STEAK

The most difficult part in preparing a stuffed flank steak is getting it rolled neatly and tied or skewered properly. I have yet to find a recipe that warns you that to "roll up tightly, jelly-roll fashion, and secure with skewers or string" is more easily said than done. Ask the butcher for a 1½- to 2-pound flank steak that is about 8 inches wide and 12 inches long. The proper size is important for easier rolling.

1 (1½- to 2-pound) flank steak
1 medium-size onion, peeled
   and quartered
1 large carrot, peeled and cut in
   pieces
2 stalks celery, cut in pieces
1 medium-size green pepper,
   seeded and quartered
5 or 6 fresh mushrooms or 1
   (4-ounce) can mushroom
   pieces, drained

Italian seasoning
Garlic powder (optional)
Freshly ground black pepper
2 tablespoons oil
1½ cups beef bouillon or
   tomato juice (low-sodium, if
   desired)

Preheat oven (if used) to 325° F.

Trim as much fat as possible from the flank steak and score it diamond fashion, about ⅜ inch deep, on one side. Set aside.

With steel knife in place, chop all vegetables, in batches if necessary, turning machine on and off until a medium chop is achieved. Mix all together in large bowl.

Place flank steak, scored side down, on work board. Sprinkle with Italian seasoning, garlic powder, and pepper to taste. Spread the vegetable filling about ¼ inch thick and not quite to the edges of the steak. Save any leftover filling to add to cooking liquid.

Starting with long edge, roll up carefully, keeping filling even. Tie with string at 1½-inch intervals and skewer ends closed.

In heavy Dutch oven, heat oil and brown flank steak over medium heat as evenly as possible. Add any leftover filling and the beef bouillon or tomato juice. There should be enough liquid to come halfway up meat. Bring to a boil, cover, and simmer on top of stove for 2½ hours or bake in oven for 2½ hours, or until very tender. Turn at least once during the cooking.

Place meat on platter and remove string and skewers. Let sit for 15 minutes.

Skim off any accumulated fat from cooking liquid. With steel knife in place, process in batches to purée vegetables. Slice meat 1 inch thick and serve with vegetable purée.

Variation: Add dry red wine to cooking liquid. Vary the stuffing—add crumbs, cottage cheese, or sapsago or Parmesan cheese, and experiment with other herbs.

SERVES 4 TO 6

EASY SWISS STEAK

2 pounds round steak cut into
  1½-inch pieces
3 tablespoons oil
½ cup parsley sprigs
1 clove garlic, peeled
2 medium-size onions, peeled
  and quartered
1 large stalk celery

1 small green pepper, seeded
  and quartered
1 (1-pound) can tomatoes
  (low-sodium, if desired),
  undrained
Salt (if allowed) or salt
  substitute, or omit
Freshly ground black pepper

Preheat oven to 325° F.

Trim meat of all visible fat and dry well. In heavy oven-going skillet or sauté pan, brown meat lightly in oil over medium heat. Drain off any excess oil after browning.

With steel knife in place, chop parsley, turning machine on and off. With machine running, drop garlic through feed tube and turn machine on and off to mince. Add onions and turn machine on and off until coarsely chopped. Add celery and green pepper and turn machine on and off. Add tomatoes and turn machine on and off to chunk. Add mixture to meat, season to taste, and stir well so meat is evenly covered. Bring to a simmer on top of stove, cover, and bake for 2½ to 3 hours, or until meat is very tender. Check to make sure there is sufficient sauce, adding water if necessary.

Variation: Add dry red wine to sauce. Add a bay leaf. Experiment!

SERVES 6 TO 8

TASTY, EASY POT ROAST

1 (3- to 4-pound) bottom round beef roast
2 tablespoons oil
2 large carrots, peeled and cut into pieces
2 stalks celery, cut into pieces
1 small onion, peeled and quartered

2 cups beef bouillon (low-sodium, if desired) or 1 package dried mushroom-onion soup mix (if allowed) and 2 cups hot water
1 cup dry red wine (optional)
Bay leaf (optional)

Preheat oven to 325° F.

Trim all fat from roast. Brown lightly in oil in heavy Dutch oven or saucepot over medium heat. Remove from pan.

With steel knife in place, chop carrots, celery, and onion coarsely, turning machine on and off until desired consistency is obtained. Add to remaining fat in pan and sauté over medium heat until vegetables start to brown. Place roast on vegetables in pan. Add bouillon or mushroom-onion soup mix and water. Liquid should come halfway up meat. Add red wine and bay leaf, if desired. Bring to a simmer on top of stove, cover, and bake about 3 to 3½ hours. Turn roast over halfway through cooking time.

Remove roast to warm place. Skim off any fat in pan, remove bay leaf, and process vegetables and cooking liquid in batches with steel knife. This will give you a delicious, natural sauce to spoon over the sliced beef.

SERVES 8 WITH LEFTOVERS

BOEUF BOURGUIGNON (or Beef Stew in Wine and elegant by any name)

---

2 to 2½ pounds lean beef
  (chuck or round steak) cut
  into 1-inch cubes
4 tablespoons oil
1 clove garlic, peeled
2 large carrots, peeled
3 medium-size onions, peeled
  and quartered
2 tablespoons flour
½ teaspoon thyme
2 small bay leaves
Pinch of sugar (or substitute)
Freshly ground black pepper to
  taste

1½ cups red Burgundy wine
1 cup or more beef bouillon
  (low-sodium, if desired)
For additional flavor, add
  1 teaspoon Kitchen Bouquet
  or Bovril, if the salt content is
  acceptable in those products
½ to 1 pound fresh
  mushrooms, sliced
2 tablespoons brandy
  (optional)
1 tablespoon oil
Lemon juice

Trim all fat from meat. Heat oil in large heavy skillet or Dutch oven with tight-fitting lid. Add meat and brown over medium heat, turning each piece carefully. This is the only time-consuming part, but important. Remove with slotted spoon and set aside.

With steel knife in place and with machine running, drop garlic through feed tube, turning machine on and off to mince. Remove to skillet or Dutch oven. Add carrots and onions to work bowl in batches and chop, turning machine on and off until coarsely chopped. Add to garlic. Sauté vegetables in remaining oil over medium heat until they begin to brown, stirring frequently. Add flour and mix well. Add seasonings, wine, and bouillon and return meat to pan. Meat should just be covered with liquid. Cover tightly and simmer slowly for at least 3 hours.

Meanwhile, with slicing disc in place, slice mushrooms. Half an hour before cooking is finished, add half the mushrooms and the brandy, if used. Sauté the remaining mushrooms in oil over medium heat for several minutes and sprinkle with lemon juice. Hold until serving time to use as a garnish.

This dish improves with age. It is easy to make at least a day ahead of serving time. Wait to sauté the mushrooms for garnish until you are serving.

SERVES 8

VEAL WITH "CRÈME AIGRE"

The "crème aigre" (or sour cream) used with this recipe is a delicious substitute for the real thing. It is added after the veal has baked to tenderness.

1½ to 2 pounds lean veal (from
    rump or shoulder)
2 tablespoons oil
1 pound mushrooms
2 tablespoons flour
½ cup chicken bouillon
    (low-sodium, if desired)
¼ cup dry white wine
Salt (if allowed) or salt
    substitute, or omit

Freshly ground black pepper
    (or white pepper)
Substitute Crème Aigre (recipe
    follows)
1 tablespoon chopped parsley
    for garnish
Lemon juice (optional)

Trim all fat from meat and cut into 1- to 1½-inch cubes. Heat oil
in heavy skillet and brown veal well over medium heat.

With slicing disc in place, slice mushrooms and add to veal.
Continue to sauté over medium heat, stirring well, for several
minutes. (You might save some of the mushroom slices, sauté in
oil over medium heat, and sprinkle with lemon juice just before
serving, to use as a garnish.)

Stir in flour, bouillon, and wine. Season to taste. Cover and
simmer gently for 1 hour.

Meanwhile, make:

SUBSTITUTE CRÈME AIGRE

1 (8-ounce) container low-fat
    creamed cottage cheese or
    pot cheese

1 tablespoon lemon juice
1 to 2 tablespoons skim milk

With steel knife in place, add cottage cheese or pot cheese. Turn
machine on and off, then let machine run until completely
smooth. Add lemon juice and 1 tablespoon skim milk, turning

machine on and off to mix well. If still too thick, particularly if you are using pot cheese, add remaining milk.

Just before veal is ready to serve, stir in ⅓ to ½ cup Substitute Crème Aigre. Heat, but do not let simmer again. Turn into serving dish and garnish with chopped parsley and sautéed mushrooms (if you saved them).

The remaining Substitute Crème Aigre can be used on salads or for dips by adding herbs and other seasonings.

SERVES 6

BAKED VEAL PATTIES

½ cup cornflake or shredded
   wheat crumbs
¼ cup parsley sprigs
1 (8-ounce) can pineapple
   packed in own juice,
   undrained
1 pound lean veal (it is more
   economical to use veal cutlets
   or veal chops—there is too
   much waste on the
   less-expensive veal cuts)

1 tablespoon oil
½ cup skim milk or evaporated
   skim milk
½ teaspoon mace
1 tablespoon lemon juice
Salt (if allowed) or salt
   substitute to taste, or omit
Freshly ground black pepper to
   taste
Paprika

Preheat oven to 350° F.

With steel knife in place, reduce enough cornflakes or shredded wheat to make ½ cup fine crumbs, turning machine on and off, then letting it whirl until desired consistency is obtained. Remove to large mixing bowl.

Chop parsley, turning machine on and off until finely minced. Add to crumbs.

Empty pineapple, with juice, into work bowl. Turn machine on and off until coarsely chopped. Set aside.

Trim veal and cut into 1-inch pieces. Process in batches, turning machine on and off until hamburger consistency is obtained. Add to crumbs with remaining ingredients except paprika and mix well with hands.

In bottom of baking dish, just large enough to hold 4 patties, spread reserved chopped pineapple. Form veal into 4 patties and place on pineapple. Sprinkle with paprika, cover tightly with foil, and bake for 30 minutes. Uncover, baste with juices, and bake 10 minutes longer.

Variation: Eliminate pineapple and place patties on lightly greased baking dish. Substitute dry white wine for lemon juice and add 1 tablespoon minced onion or scallions.

SERVES 4

VEAL BIRDS OR . . .

Like the Beef Birds or . . . (see index), you can call these by a variety of names. The stuffing can be varied. Try the following:

½ cup cornflake or bread
  crumbs
1 small onion, peeled and
  quartered
3 tablespoons oil
½ pound Simple Sausage Meat
  (see index)
⅓ cup unsweetened applesauce

1½ pounds thinly sliced veal
  (about 12 pieces)
1 tablespoon oil
1 tablespoon cornstarch
½ cup chicken bouillon
  (low-sodium, if desired)
½ cup dry white wine
Freshly ground black pepper

Preheat oven to 350° F.

With steel knife in place, reduce enough cornflakes or bread to make ½ cup coarse crumbs, turning machine on and off until desired consistency is obtained. Set aside in mixing bowl.

Add onion to work bowl. Turn machine on and off until finely minced.

Heat oil in heavy skillet and sauté onion and sausage over medium heat until lightly browned. Add to bowl with crumbs. Add applesauce and mix ingredients thoroughly.

Divide stuffing among veal slices. Roll each piece up tightly, tucking in sides. Tie with string or skewer with toothpicks.

Brown veal on all sides, over medium heat, in remaining oil in which sausage was browned (adding more if necessary). Remove browned veal rolls to oven-going casserole.

In same skillet, with 1 tablespoon oil, stir in cornstarch, bouillon, and wine, stirring briskly with whisk to ensure smooth sauce. Season to taste and pour over veal in casserole. Cover tightly and bake for 1 hour. Remove cover, baste birds well, and bake another 10 minutes.

To serve, remove string or toothpicks, arrange on serving dish, and serve with remaining sauce.

SERVES 6

SAVORY OVEN "FRIED" CHICKEN

3 pounds chicken
  parts—preferably all breast
  pieces

1½ cups cornflake crumbs
  (about 3 cups cornflakes)
¼ teaspoon garlic powder

¼ cup grated Parmesan cheese
¾ cup unsifted all-purpose
    flour
2 teaspoons paprika
Salt (if allowed) or salt
    substitute, or omit

Freshly ground black pepper
½ cup Fleischmann's Egg
    Beaters
3 tablespoons skim milk
⅓ cup margarine, plus more
    melted

Preheat oven to 400° F.

Remove skin from chicken and discard. Set chicken aside.

With steel knife in place, reduce cornflakes to crumbs, turning machine on and off, then letting it run. Add garlic powder and Parmesan cheese. Turn machine on and off to mix. Set aside in flat dish.

In separate dish, mix flour, paprika, and salt (if used) and pepper to taste.

With steel knife in place, mix Egg Beaters and milk. Set aside in third dish.

Dip pieces of chicken into flour mixture, then in Egg Beaters, and finally in crumbs. In shallow baking pan, melt ⅓ cup margarine, making certain entire surface is covered. Place chicken pieces, bone side down, in pan and drizzle with additional melted margarine. Bake uncovered for 1 hour.

This is delicious hot or cold.

SERVES 6 TO 8

BAKED CHICKEN SALAD

2 scallions, with some green
   parts
½ cup water chestnuts
1 stalk celery
1 small apple, cored, quartered,
   and peeled
2½ cups cooked chicken cut
   into 1-inch pieces

½ cup toasted, slivered
   almonds (optional)
½ cup mayonnaise (see index)
1 tablespoon lemon juice
½ cup low-fat creamed cottage
   cheese
½ cup Cheese Crumbs (see
   index)

Preheat oven to 350° F.

With steel knife in place and with machine running, drop scallions through feed tube and mince, turning machine on and off. Add water chestnuts and turn machine on and off until coarsely chopped. Set aside in mixing bowl.

Cut celery into 1-inch pieces and add with apple to work bowl. Turn machine on and off until coarsely chopped. Add to mixing bowl.

Process chicken in 2 batches, turning machine on and off for a coarse chop. Add to mixing bowl along with toasted almonds.

With steel knife in place, combine mayonnaise, lemon juice, and cottage cheese, turning machine on and off quickly. Mix thoroughly with chicken. Place in 1½-quart casserole and sprinkle with Cheese Crumbs. Bake uncovered for 20 to 25 minutes, or until just heated through.

SERVES 6

CHICKEN MOUSSE

Like the Quick Salmon Mousse, this can be a refreshing luncheon dish, a delicious addition to a buffet, or, served with Melba rounds or toast triangles, a tasty hors d'oeuvre.

1 cup evaporated skim milk, well chilled

⅔ cup firmly packed parsley sprigs

1 envelope (1 tablespoon) unflavored gelatin

½ cup boiling chicken broth (low-sodium, if desired)

2 tablespoons lemon juice

3 scallions, white part only, cut in pieces

½ pound boneless cooked chicken breasts (1½ cups cut into 1-inch pieces)

¾ cup mayonnaise (see index)

¼ cup blanched, slivered almonds (optional)

Cucumber Mayonnaise (recipe follows)

Watercress or parsley sprigs for garnish

Cherry tomatoes for garnish

Place milk in freezer until ice crystals form.

With steel knife in place, chop parsley, turning machine on and off, and set aside.

Empty gelatin into work bowl. Add boiling chicken broth, lemon juice, and scallions. Blend, turning on and off until scallions are completely liquefied. Add chicken and mayonnaise and blend until smooth. Add reserved parsley and turn on and off until evenly distributed. Pour in chilled milk and process for 20 seconds. Add almonds, if using, and turn machine on and off.

Pour mixture into lightly oiled 4-cup mold and refrigerate until firm.

CUCUMBER MAYONNAISE

½ cucumber, peeled and seeded   *¾ cup mayonnaise (see index)*

With shredding disc in place, shred cucumber. Drain well, pressing out as much liquid as possible. Mix with mayonnaise.

To serve, unmold mousse onto serving platter and surround with watercress or parsley sprigs and cherry tomatoes. Serve Cucumber Mayonnaise in separate bowl.

SERVES 4 TO 6 AS A LUNCHEON DISH OR 10 TO 12 AS AN HORS D'OEUVRE

BAKED CHICKEN LOAF

1½ cups cornflake, shredded wheat, or cracker crumbs
⅓ cup parsley sprigs
1 pound boneless cooked chicken (3 cups cut into 1-inch pieces)
1 small onion, peeled and quartered
1 small stalk celery
1 pimiento, drained
Salt (if allowed) or salt substitute, or omit

Freshly ground black pepper
½ cup chicken bouillon (low-sodium, if desired)
½ cup evaporated skim milk
2 tablespoons margarine
½ cup Fleischmann's Egg Beaters or 2 egg whites, slightly beaten
Mushroom Sauce (recipe follows)

Preheat oven to 350° F.

With steel knife in place, reduce enough cornflakes or other to make 1½ cups crumbs. Turn machine on and off, then let run until desired consistency is obtained. Set aside in large mixing bowl.

Add parsley and turn machine on and off until finely minced. Add to mixing bowl with crumbs.

Using 1 cup chicken pieces at a time, turn machine on and off until coarsely chopped. Add to mixing bowl.

Add onion, celery, and pimiento to work bowl. Turn machine on and off until finely chopped. Season mixture to taste.

Warm bouillon, milk, and margarine over low heat. Add to chicken mixture. With steel knife in place, whirl Egg Beaters or egg whites for 5 seconds. Add to chicken mixture. Blend entire mixture with hands. Pack in well-greased 8½″×4½″×2½″ loaf pan. Bake uncovered for 1 hour.

Serve with:

MUSHROOM SAUCE

¼ pound fresh mushrooms or
   1 small can sliced mushrooms
   (low-sodium, if desired),
   drained
1 tablespoon oil
1 tablespoon flour

1 cup chicken bouillon
   (low-sodium, if desired)
White pepper
1 pimiento, chopped
2 tablespoons dry white wine
   (optional)

With slicing disc in place, slice mushrooms. Heat oil in skillet and sauté mushrooms over medium heat until limp. Add flour and mix well. Stir in chicken bouillon and continue stirring until thickened. Add additional seasonings, pimiento, and wine.

SERVES 4 TO 6

EASY SALMON SANDWICHES

#1

1 stalk celery
½ small green pepper, seeded
1 (7¾-ounce) can salmon,
    drained

Mayonnaise (see index)
Salt (if allowed) or salt
    substitute, or omit
Freshly ground black pepper

With steel knife in place, cut celery into pieces and add to work bowl with green pepper. Turn machine on and off until finely minced. Add salmon and turn machine on and off twice. Add a tablespoon or more of mayonnaise and salt (if used) and pepper to taste and turn machine on and off to mix.

MAKES ABOUT 1½ CUPS OR ENOUGH FOR 4 SANDWICHES
(ON THINLY SLICED BREAD)

#2

½ cucumber, peeled and seeded
1 (7¾-ounce) can salmon,
    drained
½ teaspoon dried dill weed
Mayonnaise (see index) to bind
    mixture—about 1 tablespoon

Salt (if allowed) or salt
    substitute to taste, or omit
Freshly ground black pepper to
    taste

With shredding disc in place, shred cucumber and drain well.
    With steel knife in place, add cucumber and remaining ingredients. Turn machine on and off just to mix.

MAKES ABOUT 1½ CUPS OR ENOUGH FOR 3 TO 4
SANDWICHES (ON THINLY SLICED BREAD)

TUNA SANDWICHES

½ cup walnuts
1 (7-ounce) can tuna in water,
  drained

1 teaspoon lemon juice
Mayonnaise (see index) to
  moisten—about 3 tablespoons

With steel knife in place, chop walnuts, turning machine on and off until coarsely chopped. Add tuna, lemon juice, and mayonnaise. Turn machine on and off until just blended. Add more mayonnaise if needed.

MAKES ABOUT 1½ CUPS OR ENOUGH FOR 3 TO 4
SANDWICHES (ON THINLY SLICED BREAD)

Variation:

1 cucumber
Curry powder to taste

Chopped parsley or watercress
  for garnish

With slicing disc, slice cucumber, drain, and set aside. Add curry powder to original recipe, above.

Spread thin layer of margarine on thinly sliced bread. Cover with cucumber slices and add tuna mixture. Serve open-face, garnished with chopped parsley or watercress.

MAKES 6 TO 8 OPEN-FACE SANDWICHES

LEFTOVER BEEF SANDWICHES

From the Tasty, Easy Pot Roast (see index), a delicious sandwich can be made with any leftovers.

For one sandwich just chop 3 ounces leftover pot roast with steel knife in place, turning machine on and off quickly to retain texture. Mix with 1 teaspoon chili sauce (low-sodium, if desired) and 1 teaspoon mayonnaise (or enough to moisten). Add freshly ground pepper to taste and the sandwich is ready.

MAKES 1 SANDWICH

Breads

About Breads

The rewards of homemade bread are many on this diet, not the least of which is the fragrance of the bread while baking.

With the food processor to do the initial mixing and kneading, yeast breads can be ready for rising in minutes.

Quick breads, Allowable Pâte à Chou, Carl Sontheimer's Skinny Crêpes, and others are quickly made.

Calories must be taken into consideration, but the following selective group of recipes was developed for a low-cholesterol, low-sodium, low-fat diet. Let the food processor do the work and make any meal an occasion.

EASY WHITE BREAD

According to ancient legend, the Egyptians believed in thorough kneading. The historian Herodotus says, "Dough they knead with their feet. . . ." It is much easier and more efficient in the food processor!

½ cup skim milk
½ cup water
4 teaspoons margarine
1 tablespoon sugar (or substitute)

1 envelope active dry yeast
2⅔ to 3 cups unsifted all-purpose flour
1 teaspoon salt (if allowed) or salt substitute, or omit

In small saucepan, warm first 3 ingredients to 105–115° F. Remove from heat and add sugar and yeast. Let stand until yeast dissolves, about 4 to 5 minutes.

With steel knife in place, add 2⅔ cups flour and salt (if used) to work bowl. Add half the proofed yeast and turn machine on and off 3 times. Add remaining yeast and turn machine on and off until ball of dough forms. It may be necessary to scrape down sides of bowl. The dough should be sticky but not wet. If too sticky, add remaining flour, a tablespoon at a time, processing with on and off turns after each addition. Let machine run for 50 to 60 seconds to knead dough. Flour your hands and remove dough carefully from work bowl. Work dough with your hands for a minute or so.

Place dough in oiled bowl, turning so that oiled surface is on top. Cover with damp cloth and let rise in warm place (80° F.) until doubled (about 1¼ hours). Punch dough down, form into loaf, and place in greased 6-cup loaf pan. Let rise again, covered, until nearly doubled in bulk (about 45 to 55 minutes).

Preheat oven to 375° F. Bake for about 40 to 45 minutes until nicely browned and hollow-sounding when tapped, or until internal temperature reaches 210° F.

Turn out of pan immediately and cool on wire rack.

MAKES 1 LOAF

BREAD OR ROLLS ALL'OLIO

This has been a very satisfying white bread and roll recipe. It can be made salt-free and goes together quickly in the food processor.

1 package active dry yeast
2 tablespoons sugar (or substitute)
1 cup warm water (105–115° F.)
3¼ to 3½ cups unsifted all-purpose flour

1 teaspoon salt (if allowed) or salt substitute, or omit
¼ cup oil (try olive oil for a different flavor)
Fleischmann's Egg Beaters for glaze

Add yeast and sugar to warm water and let stand until dissolved, about 4 to 5 minutes.

With steel knife in place, add 3¼ cups flour and salt (if used) to work bowl. Turn machine on and off twice. Add oil and turn machine on and off several times, scraping down sides if necessary, and making certain oil is well incorporated. Add half of yeast mixture and turn machine on and off 4 times. Add remaining yeast mixture. Turn machine on and off until ball of dough forms. The dough should be slightly sticky. If necessary, add additional flour, a tablespoon at a time, turning machine on and off to incorporate flour. Let machine run for 50 to 60 seconds to knead dough.

Flour your hands and remove dough carefully from work bowl. Work dough with your hands for a minute or so.

Place dough in oiled bowl, turning so that all surfaces are oiled. Cover with damp cloth and let rise in warm place (80°F.) until doubled (about 1¼ hours). Punch dough down, turn out on lightly floured surface, and let rest for 5 minutes.

To make 1 loaf of bread, form dough into loaf and place in 6-cup loaf pan. Let rise again, covered, until nearly doubled in bulk (about 45 to 55 minutes).

Preheat oven to 375°F. Carefully paint top of loaf with Egg Beaters and bake for 40 minutes, or until nicely browned and hollow-sounding when tapped, or until internal temperature reaches 210°F. Turn out of pan immediately and cool on wire rack.

To make rolls, divide dough into about 18 even pieces. Roll each piece into a rope about 6 inches long and ½ inch in diameter. Tie carefully in a loose knot and place 2 inches apart on lightly greased baking sheets. (Or shape into crescents or other shapes.) Brush tops lightly with Egg Beaters, cover with damp cloth, and let rise again until doubled. To avoid damp cloth touching rolls during second rising, place a water goblet at corners of baking sheets and drape cloth over the goblets.

Preheat oven to 375° F. When doubled in bulk, bake for about 20 minutes, or until nicely browned. Remove from baking sheet and cool on wire rack.

MAKES 1 LARGE LOAF OF BREAD OR 18 OR MORE ROLLS

HERBED BREAD STICKS

1 package active dry yeast
1 cup warm water
   (105–115° F.)
2 tablespoons sugar (or
   substitute)
2 teaspoons caraway seeds
3 to 3¼ cups unsifted
   all-purpose flour

1 teaspoon salt (if allowed) or
   salt substitute, or omit
1 tablespoon margarine
Fleischmann's Egg Beaters for
   glaze
Caraway seeds (optional)

Add yeast and sugar to warm water and let stand until dissolved, about 4 to 5 minutes.

With steel knife in place, add the 2 teaspoons caraway seeds, 3 cups flour, and salt (if used) to work bowl. Turn machine on and off twice. Add margarine and turn machine on and off 4 or 5 times, scraping down sides if necessary. Add half of yeast mixture and turn machine on and off 3 times. Add remaining yeast and turn machine on and off until ball of dough forms. If mixture is too sticky, add remaining flour, a tablespoon at a time, turning machine on and off to incorporate. Let machine run for 50 to 60 seconds to knead dough.

Flour your hands and remove dough carefully from work bowl. Work dough with your hands for a minute or so.

Place dough in oiled bowl, turning so that all surfaces are oiled. Cover with damp cloth and let rise in warm place (80° F.) until doubled (about 1¼ hours).

Punch dough down, divide into 2 equal portions, and, on a lightly floured cloth, roll each half into a roll about 12 inches long. Cut each roll into 12 even pieces. Roll each piece to form a rope about 12 inches long and ⅓ inch in diameter. Place on greased baking sheets about 1 inch apart, brush lightly with Egg Beaters, and sprinkle with additional caraway seeds, if desired. Place a water goblet at each corner of baking sheets and drape damp cloth over—this will prevent the cloth from touching the rolls during their second rising (this takes about 45 minutes).

Preheat oven to 400° F. When doubled in bulk, bake for 15 to 20 minutes. Remove from baking sheets and cool on wire racks.

Variation: Substitute other herbs for the caraway seeds.

MAKES 24 BREAD STICKS

CINNAMON SWIRL ORANGE BREAD

1 package active dry yeast
1 tablespoon sugar (or substitute)
¼ cup warm water (105–115° F.)
1 tablespoon orange rind (thin zest from 1 medium-size orange)
2 tablespoons sugar (or substitute)
2½ cups unsifted all-purpose flour

1 teaspoon salt (if allowed) or salt substitute, or omit
3 tablespoons margarine
⅔ cup orange juice (about)
¼ cup sugar (or substitute)
1½ teaspoons cinnamon
1 teaspoon water
1 tablespoon melted margarine
Cinnamon (optional)
Sugar (optional)

Add yeast and 1 tablespoon sugar to warm water and let stand until dissolved, about 4 to 5 minutes.

With steel knife in place, add orange zest and the 2 tablespoons sugar to work bowl. Turn machine on and off, then let run until orange zest is finely minced. Add flour, salt (if used), and margarine and process for about 20 seconds. Add yeast mixture and process for about 5 seconds.

With machine running, pour half the orange juice through feed tube. Then drizzle additional orange juice through feed tube just until ball of dough forms. Let machine run for 50 to 60 seconds to knead, or turn out on lightly floured board and knead until smooth—2 to 3 minutes.

Flour your hands and remove dough carefully from work bowl. Place in oiled bowl, turning so that all surfaces are oiled. Cover with damp towel and let rise in warm place (about 80° F.) until doubled in bulk (about 1¼ hours).

Mix together the ¼ cup sugar and the cinnamon.

Punch dough down, cover, and let rest 10 minutes. On lightly floured surface, roll out dough to a rectangle about 15×7 inches, ½ inch thick. Sprinkle sugar-cinnamon mixture over dough and sprinkle with 1 teaspoon water. Smooth with spatula. Roll up like jelly roll and seal edge. Place seam side down in greased 8½- to 9-inch loaf pan. Cover and let rise again until double (about 45 minutes).

Preheat oven to 375° F. Just before baking, brush loaf with melted margarine and sprinkle with additional cinnamon-sugar, if desired. Bake for 30 minutes. Turn out onto wire rack to cool.

MAKES 1 LOAF

POPOVERS

It is important that these be started in a cold oven. In pre-low-cholesterol days, my favorite recipe called for a hot oven. When experimenting with a no-egg-yolk recipe, I followed the hot-oven procedure. The result was an interesting, beautifully formed, delicately browned flat popover.

3 egg whites, at room
    temperature
1½ tablespoons melted
    margarine
1 tablespoon oil
¼ teaspoon butter flavoring
    (optional but good)

1 cup skim milk mixed with
    2 tablespoons dry skim milk
1 cup unsifted all-purpose flour
Pinch of sugar (optional)
½ teaspoon salt (if allowed) or
    salt substitute, or omit

Grease 8 custard cups or popover pans very well.

With steel knife in place, add egg whites to processor bowl. Turn machine on and off 3 or 4 times to whip the whites slightly. Add melted margarine, oil, butter flavoring, if used, and milk. Turn machine on and off, then let run for 5 seconds. Add flour and sugar and salt (if used). Turn machine on and off, then let run for 5 more seconds.

Fill greased cups two-thirds full. Place in cold oven. Turn oven to 400° F. and bake for 50 to 60 minutes, or until nicely browned. If popovers should start browning too quickly, reduce heat to 350° F. for last 20 minutes.

MAKES 8 POPOVERS

CORIANDER BISCUITS

The flavor of coriander in these biscuits is the result of trying to duplicate the taste of some biscuits often served at one of our favorite restaurants. I have since learned that most of the coriander grown in the United States ends up in the gin bottle. Little wonder it adds an interesting flavor to these biscuits.

2 cups unsifted all-purpose flour
2 teaspoons sugar (or
  substitute)
3 teaspoons baking powder (if
  using low-sodium, use 4½
  teaspoons)

1 teaspoon ground coriander
½ teaspoon salt (if allowed) or
  salt substitute, or omit
5 tablespoons margarine
¾ cup evaporated skim milk

Preheat oven to 450° F.

With steel knife in place, add all dry ingredients. Turn machine on and off 3 times to aerate. Add margarine and turn machine on and off until mealy. Add milk and turn machine on and off quickly, just until flour disappears.

Flour your hands and carefully remove dough from work bowl. Shape into a ball and knead a few times with your hands. On lightly floured surface, pat dough out to ½ inch thickness and cut biscuits with 1½-inch cutter.

Place 1 inch apart on lightly greased cookie sheet and bake for 10 to 12 minutes, or until lightly browned.

Variation: Omit coriander and try other herbs or spices.

MAKES 12 BISCUITS

POPPY SEED BREAD

⅓ cup poppy seeds	⅓ cup Fleischmann's Egg
1¼ cups evaporated skim milk	Beaters
1 teaspoon grated lemon rind	2½ cups unsifted all-purpose
(3 strips lemon zest)	flour
½ cup sugar (use half regular	1 tablespoon baking powder (if
and half substitute)	using low-sodium, increase to
⅓ cup margarine	1½ tablespoons)

Preheat oven to 350° F.

Mix poppy seeds with milk and let stand overnight or at least 6 hours.

With steel knife in place, cut lemon zest into pieces and add to work bowl with half the sugar. Turn machine on and off, then let run until lemon is thoroughly minced. Add remaining sugar and the margarine and turn machine on and off until well creamed.

Add poppy seeds with milk and Egg Beaters. Turn machine on and off to mix well, then let machine run for 5 seconds.

Mix flour with baking powder and add to work bowl. Turn machine on and off until dry ingredients are well incorporated.

Turn into well-greased and lightly floured 9″×5″×3″ loaf pan. Bake for 1 hour, or until it tests done with a cake tester. Turn out onto wire rack and cool completely.

MAKES 1 LOAF

QUICK APRICOT-BANANA BREAD

¼ cup chopped walnuts
  (optional)
⅔ cup pure apricot preserves
1 medium-size banana, cut into
  pieces
¼ cup oil
¼ cup evaporated skim milk
½ cup Fleischmann's Egg
  Beaters

½ teaspoon salt (if allowed) or
  salt substitute, or omit
2 cups unsifted all-purpose flour
2 teaspoons baking powder (if
  using low-sodium, increase to
  3 teaspoons)
Apricot-Cheese Spread
  (recipe follows; optional)

Preheat oven to 350° F.

With steel knife in place, chop walnuts coarsely, turning machine on and off. Set aside.

Add next 5 ingredients to work bowl. Turn machine on and off, scraping down sides if necessary, then let machine run for about 6 seconds.

Combine dry ingredients and add to work bowl with reserved nuts. Turn machine on and off until flour disappears, again scraping down sides if necessary, then let machine run for 3 seconds.

Turn into well-greased 9"×5"×3" loaf pan or three 4½"×2¾"×2½" loaf pans. Bake for 50 minutes for large loaf and 35 minutes for small loaves. Turn out onto wire rack and cool completely.

MAKES 1 LARGE LOAF OR 3 SMALL LOAVES

APRICOT-CHEESE SPREAD

For a special-occasion spread to use with this bread, soak ½ cup dried apricots in water overnight. Drain, cut into pieces, and add to work bowl with 1 cup low-fat creamed cottage cheese. Turn machine on and off until apricots are coarsely chopped. Delicious!

MAKES ABOUT 1⅓ CUPS

CORN BREAD

---

2 egg whites	½ cup unsifted all-purpose
1½ cups buttermilk	flour
¼ cup oil	2 tablespoons sugar (use half
½ teaspoon butter flavoring	substitute)
1½ cups cornmeal*	½ teaspoon baking soda

Preheat oven to 425° F.

With steel knife in place, add egg whites to work bowl. Turn machine on and off, then let run for 5 seconds. Add buttermilk, oil, and butter flavoring and turn machine on and off 3 or 4 times.

Add remaining ingredients and turn machine on and off just until the dry ingredients disappear. Pour into greased and floured 9-inch-square pan and bake for 20 to 25 minutes. Serve hot.

If you have any left over, split, cover with thin layer of margarine, and run under broiler.

MAKES 12 PIECES

* If using white cornmeal, you can add a drop or two of yellow food coloring with the liquid ingredients, if desired.

QUICK BREAKFAST COFFEE CAKE

¼ cup chopped walnuts

2¾ cups unsifted all-purpose flour

1½ teaspoons baking powder (if using low-sodium, increase to 2¼ teaspoons)

1½ teaspoons crushed cardamom seed

½ teaspoon instant lemon peel

1 cup sugar (use half substitute)

½ cup margarine

1⅓ cups evaporated skim milk

2 tablespoons sugar (or substitute)

½ teaspoon cinnamon

Preheat oven to 375° F.

With steel knife in place, add walnuts to work bowl and chop coarsely, turning machine on and off. Set aside.

Add next 5 ingredients to work bowl. Turn machine on and off several times to mix and aerate ingredients. Cut margarine into 6 or 8 pieces and add to flour mixture. Turn machine on and off several times until mixture resembles cornmeal. Add milk and turn machine on and off just enough to mix well.

Turn into well-greased 9-inch-square pan. Mix the 2 tablespoons sugar and the cinnamon and sprinkle over top. Sprinkle reserved nuts over that. With a spatula or silver knife, swirl cinnamon and nuts gently through the batter.

Bake for 35 to 40 minutes. Serve warm.

MAKES 12 SMALL SERVINGS

ALLOWABLE PÂTE À CHOU

½ cup water

4 tablespoons margarine
  (salt-free, if desired)

½ cup unsifted all-purpose
  flour

1 teaspoon sugar (optional—if
  using as dessert puffs)

4 tablespoons Fleischmann's
  Egg Beaters (remove from
  refrigerator about an hour
  before using)

Preheat oven to 400° F.

Heat water and margarine to a boil. Add flour and sugar (if used) and stir vigorously until ball forms. Cook for a minute or two more, stirring constantly. With steel knife in place, add mixture to work bowl. With machine running, add 2 tablespoons Egg Beaters and let machine run for 5 seconds. Add the remaining Egg Beaters and let machine continue to run for another 10 seconds.

Drop dough by rounded teaspoons 1½ inches apart on ungreased baking sheet. Bake for 15 minutes at 400° F. Reduce heat to 350° F. and bake for 15 minutes more. Don't open the oven until the last 5 minutes of baking time.

To ensure dry puffs, poke or spear each one to let steam escape. Cut and fill with your choice of filling.

Variation: Add 1 tablespoon grated Parmesan cheese along with the Egg Beaters. This makes an interesting flavor when used for hors d'oeuvre.

MAKES ABOUT 30 PUFFS

CARL SONTHEIMER'S SKINNY CRÊPES

When I told Carl Sontheimer I was not including a crêpe recipe in my book, primarily because of the calories involved, he offered to sell me the following (about 25 calories per crêpe):

1 egg white
½ cup unsifted all-purpose flour
⅓ cup water
⅛ teaspoon (about) baking powder (low-sodium, if desired)—this is not essential but produces a more tender crêpe

Sugar—also not essential, but a pinch or so will aid the browning process

With steel knife in place, add egg white to work bowl. Turn machine on and off several times. Add remaining ingredients. Turn machine on and off, then let run about 5 seconds. Allow batter to sit for 10 minutes.

Using a pastry brush, lightly oil a 5-inch crêpe pan or skillet. Keep more oil handy for additional crêpes. Heat skillet until drop of water sizzles and bounces off. Using about 1½ tablespoons of batter, pour into skillet and quickly tilt pan so entire bottom is covered. Return to heat and cook over moderately high heat until crêpe looks dry. This takes only a few seconds. Loosen with spatula and turn to cook underside briefly. Remove and repeat with remaining batter. You will get 4 or 5 small crêpes.

Spread with small amount of preserves or cottage cheese, roll, and serve.

Variation: Crêpes Citron: Spread crêpes with margarine, sprinkle with a little sugar, and moisten with lemon juice. Roll up, place seam side down in baking dish, sprinkle with a little more sugar, and heat briefly in moderate oven.

MAKES 4 TO 5 SMALL CRÊPES

FRENCH TOAST OR PAIN PERDU

French toast is known as pain perdu in some parts of the country, since it is believed the bread loses its identity when dipped in the egg mixture and sautéed. The following 2 recipes are low in cholesterol, but watch the calorie count and triglyceride level with any preserves, honey, or syrup used.

#1

¾ cup Fleischmann's Egg
   Beaters
½ cup skim milk
Pinch of sugar (or substitute)
½ teaspoon nutmeg

6 slices bread, slightly
   stale—whole wheat bread is
   delicious!
2 tablespoons margarine or oil

With plastic or steel knife in place, add all ingredients except bread and margarine to work bowl. Turn machine on and off, then let run for 5 seconds. Pour mixture into flat dish, large enough to accommodate the bread slices. Dip bread slices into mixture and let soak for a minute or two.

In heavy skillet, heat margarine or oil. Sauté bread slices over medium heat until golden brown and crisp on both sides. Additional margarine or oil may be needed.

Serve with your choice of spreads, remembering the calories.

MAKES 6 SLICES

#2

3 egg whites

1 tablespoon oil

3 tablespoons evaporated skim milk

Yellow food coloring (a drop or two for color, if desired)

⅛ teaspoon nutmeg or cinnamon

Pinch of sugar (or substitute)

Pinch of salt (if allowed) or salt substitute, or omit

4 slices slightly stale bread

2 tablespoons margarine or oil

With plastic or steel knife in place, add all ingredients except bread and margarine. Turn machine on and off, then let run for about 8 seconds. Pour mixture into flat dish, large enough to accommodate bread slices.

Heat margarine or oil in heavy skillet. Dip bread slices into mixture and let soak for a minute or two. Sauté in skillet over medium heat, turning occasionally, until browned and crisp on both sides.

Serve with your choice of spreads, remembering the calories.

MAKES 4 SLICES

Desserts

About Desserts

Like the hors d'oeuvre and bread chapters, the dessert chapter is slim but selective. Sugar, except for calorie content, contributes little nutritive value to the diet. In addition, tests indicate that excessive consumption of sugar increases triglycerides.

The following recipes, however, are a welcome change from the usually recommended gelatin dessert, fruit ice, or plain pudding made with skim milk. They will all satisfy the dieter's sweet tooth within the limits of the diet as well as keeping guests and/or other members of the family healthy and satisfied.

BUTTERSCOTCH SLICES

½ cup well-toasted almonds

¼ cup margarine

1½ tablespoons oil

½ cup dark (or light) brown sugar (or substitute)

½ cup granulated sugar (or substitute)

2 tablespoons Fleischmann's Egg Beaters

1½ teaspoons vanilla

1½ cups unsifted all-purpose flour

¼ teaspoon salt (if allowed) or salt substitute, or omit

½ teaspoon baking powder (if using low-sodium, increase to ¾ teaspoon)

With steel knife in place, add almonds to work bowl and chop coarsely, turning machine on and off. Set aside.

Add margarine, oil, and sugars to bowl. Turn machine on and off to cream thoroughly. Add Egg Beaters and vanilla and turn machine on and off 3 times. Combine flour, salt (if used), and baking powder. Add to work bowl with reserved almonds. Turn machine on and off until flour mixture disappears.

Shape dough into roll about 1½ inches in diameter. Chill thoroughly, at least 3 to 4 hours.

When ready to bake, preheat oven to 400° F. Slice cookies about ⅛ inch thick and place 1 inch apart on lightly oiled cookie sheet. Bake for 10 to 12 minutes, or until lightly browned. Cool on wire racks.

MAKES ABOUT 2 DOZEN

PEANUT BUTTER COOKIES

⅓ cup well-toasted almonds or
   ⅓ cup walnuts (almonds
   give better flavor here)
½ cup dark (or light) brown
   sugar (or substitute)
¼ cup granulated sugar (or
   substitute)
2 tablespoons oil
2 tablespoons margarine
¼ cup low-sodium peanut
   butter (see index)—or
   regular, if desired

2 egg whites
1 cup unsifted all-purpose flour
¼ teaspoon salt (if allowed) or
   salt substitute, or omit
1 teaspoon baking power (if
   using low-sodium, increase to
   1½ teaspoons)

Preheat oven to 375° F.

With steel knife in place, add almonds or walnuts to work bowl. Turn machine on and off until a fairly fine texture is achieved. Set aside.

Add sugars, oil, and margarine to work bowl. Turn machine on and off to cream well. Add peanut butter, turning machine on and off to blend. Add egg whites, turn machine on and off, then let run for about 8 seconds. Combine flour, salt (if used), and baking powder. Add to work bowl with reserved nuts. Turn machine on and off just until flour disappears.

Drop dough from teaspoon onto greased cookie sheets, about 1 inch apart, flattening with fork dipped in flour (make a crisscross pattern). Bake for 10 to 12 minutes, or until lightly browned. Cool for a minute or two before removing from cookie sheet. Finish cooling on wire racks.

MAKES ABOUT 36

BROWNIES

½ cup walnuts
1 cup firmly packed light
   brown sugar
¼ cup oil
1 teaspoon vanilla
¼ cup Fleischmann's Egg
   Beaters
½ cup unsifted all-purpose
   flour

2 tablespoons unsweetened
   cocoa
½ teaspoon baking powder (if
   using low-sodium, increase to
   ¾ teaspoon)
⅛ teaspoon salt (if allowed) or
   salt substitute, or omit

Preheat oven to 350° F.

With steel knife in place, add walnuts to work bowl and chop, turning machine on and off until desired consistency is obtained. Set aside.

Add sugar and oil to bowl and process until lumps are gone from sugar and mixture is smooth. Add vanilla and Egg Beaters, turning machine on and off several times to mix well.

Add dry ingredients all at once with reserved walnuts. Turn machine on and off until dry ingredients have disappeared.

Spread mixture in well-greased 8-inch-square pan and bake for 30 minutes. Cool in pan on wire rack before cutting.

MAKES 12 SMALL BROWNIES

GRANDMOTHER'S SPRITZ

Included here only because you CAN make them without real butter, and if you don't know, they taste just as good.

1 cup margarine
⅔ cup sugar
¼ cup Fleischmann's Egg Beaters
1 teaspoon vanilla
2½ cups unsifted all-purpose flour*

¼ teaspoon baking powder (if using low-sodium, increase to ⅜ teaspoon)
Pinch of salt (if allowed) or salt substitute, or omit

Preheat oven to 400° F.

With steel knife in place, cut margarine into chunks and add to work bowl with sugar. Turn machine on and off, then let machine run until mixture is light and fluffy. Add Egg Beaters and vanilla and turn machine on and off to mix well. Scrape down bowl, if necessary.

Combine dry ingredients and add to work bowl. Turn machine on and off just until flour disappears and dough is well mixed.

* You may need to add a little more flour to make the dough stiff enough to work well in the cookie press. It will depend on the consistency of the flour.

Using the star disc of a cookie press, form dough into circles about 1 inch in diameter, 1 inch apart, on ungreased cookie sheets. Bake for 7 to 10 minutes, or until lightly browned. Cool on wire racks.

MAKES OVER 6 DOZEN SMALL COOKIES, WHICH FREEZE WELL

POUND CAKE—LEMON AND OTHER

This makes a delicious, small, firm-textured cake, the flavoring of which can be varied.

1 teaspoon grated lemon rind
(3 strips of lemon zest)
¾ cup sugar (use half regular
and half substitute, if
desired)
½ cup margarine
⅔ cup Fleischmann's Egg
Beaters
¼ cup evaporated skim milk

1 teaspoon vanilla
1⅓ cups unsifted all-purpose
flour
½ teaspoon baking powder (if
using low-sodium, increase to
¾ teaspoon)
Pinch of salt (if allowed) or salt
substitute, or omit

Preheat oven to 350° F.

With steel knife in place, add lemon zest and ¼ cup sugar to work bowl. Turn machine on and off, then let run until finely minced. Add remaining sugar and margarine, cut into pieces. Turn on and off until well creamed. Add Egg Beaters, skim milk, and vanilla. Turn machine on and off, then let run for 5 seconds. Scrape down bowl, if necessary.

Combine dry ingredients and add to work bowl. Turn machine on and off until flour mixture completely disappears.

Grease and flour a 4-cup bundt pan. Turn cake mixture into pan and bake for 50 minutes. Cool for 5 minutes, then turn out onto wire rack and cool completely. Keeps well in refrigerator and freezes well.

Variations: Use orange rind instead of lemon rind.

Reduce lemon rind to ½ teaspoon, eliminate vanilla, and add 1½ teaspoons crushed cardamom seed with dry ingredients. One tablespoon rum or 1 teaspoon rum flavoring can be substituted for vanilla.

PUMPKIN CHEESE CAKE

⅓ cup graham cracker crumbs
  (4 or 5 squares)
2 cups low-fat creamed cottage
  cheese
½ cup dark (or light) brown
  sugar

½ teaspoon cinnamon
½ teaspoon mace
2 tablespoons dark rum
½ cup Fleischmann's Egg
  Beaters
1 cup canned pumpkin

Preheat oven to 350° F.

With steel knife in place, break 4 or 5 graham cracker squares into work bowl. Turn machine on and off, then let run until finely chopped. Set aside.

Add cottage cheese to bowl and process until absolutely smooth, scraping down sides if necessary to ensure velvety texture. Add brown sugar, cinnamon, mace, and rum and process, turning machine on and off until sugar is well incorporated. Add

Egg Beaters and pumpkin, turning machine on and off twice, then letting machine run for 8 seconds.

Sprinkle bottom of an 8-inch springform pan with reserved graham cracker crumbs (saving a teaspoon to sprinkle on top). Pour pumpkin mixture into pan and bake for about 55 minutes, or until a knife inserted in center comes out clean. Just before filling is done, prepare topping:

½ cup low-fat creamed cottage cheese	1 teaspoon vanilla
1 teaspoon lemon juice	1 teaspoon sugar (or substitute)
	1 tablespoon skim milk

With steel knife in place, add all ingredients to work bowl and process until smooth, scraping down sides if necessary. If topping seems too thick (it should be the consistency of sour cream), add a little more skim milk.

When cake tests done, remove from oven and spread topping over entire surface. Sprinkle with reserved crumbs and bake another 6 minutes. Cool on wire rack, then refrigerate until well chilled, at least 4 hours.

To serve, run knife around edge of cake and remove rim of springform pan. Leave cake on springform bottom to serve.

MAKES 8 SERVINGS

APPLE DESSERT

1 cup graham cracker crumbs
  (about 12 squares)
1/4 cup chopped walnuts
1 teaspoon grated orange rind
  (2 or 3 strips of orange zest)
1/2 cup sugar (use half regular
  and half substitute, if
  desired)
2 tablespoons oil

4 or 5 tart cooking apples,
  peeled and cored
1/4 cup sugar (use half regular
  and half substitute, if
  desired)
1/2 teaspoon mace or nutmeg
1/4 teaspoon cinnamon
Vanilla-flavored yogurt
  (optional)

Preheat oven to 350° F.

With steel knife in place, crumble graham crackers into work bowl and reduce to fine crumbs. Set aside. Add walnuts and chop coarsely, turning machine on and off. Set aside with crumbs. Add orange zest and the 1/2 cup sugar to bowl. Turn machine on and off, then let run until finely grated. Return crumbs and nuts to bowl, add oil, and turn machine on and off to mix. Set mixture aside.

With slicing disc in place, cut apples to fit feed tube and slice. Arrange in greased 9-inch pie pan or square baking dish. Sprinkle with mixture of the 1/4 cup sugar and the mace or nutmeg and cinnamon. Sprinkle reserved crumb mixture over apples and bake for about 40 minutes, or until apples are tender and topping is browned. Delicious hot or cold, topped with a dollop of vanilla-flavored yogurt.

SERVES 6

APPLE AND PEAR DESSERT

1 cup cornflake crumbs (about
  2 cups cornflakes)
1 teaspoon grated lemon rind
  (3 strips of lemon zest)
½ cup sugar (use half regular
  and half substitute, if
  desired)

½ teaspoon nutmeg or mace
Pinch of salt, if desired
3 or 4 fresh ripe pears, peeled
  and cored
3 tart apples, peeled and cored
3 tablespoons margarine
Yogurt (optional)

Preheat oven to 350° F.

With steel knife in place, reduce cornflakes to fine crumbs and set aside in mixing bowl.

Place lemon zest and sugar in work bowl. Turn machine on and off, then let run until reduced to fine consistency. Add to crumbs in mixing bowl with nutmeg or mace and salt (if used). Mix together thoroughly.

With slicing disc in place, cut pears and apples to fit feed tube and slice. In a 1-quart greased baking dish, combine one third of the fruit, sprinkle over one third cornflake mixture, and dot with 1 tablespoon margarine. Repeat twice more, using remaining ingredients.

Bake for 1 hour, or until fruit is tender. Serve hot or cold, with a dollop of yogurt.

SERVES 6

CRÈME DE MENTHE PEAR FREEZE

1 (1-pound) can pear halves or
  sliced pears (dietetic, if
  desired), frozen in unopened
  can

1 teaspoon crème de menthe
  extract (or more, to taste)
1 to 2 drops green food
  coloring

Run warm water over can of pears and remove pears from can. Chop into pieces with large knife.

With steel knife in place, add pears to work bowl with flavoring and food coloring. Turn machine on and off several times, then let machine run until mixture is creamy. Serve immediately or refreeze.

SERVES 3 OR 4

PEACH-ALMOND FREEZE

1 (1-pound) can sliced peaches
  (dietetic, if desired), frozen
  in unopened can

½ teaspoon almond extract
¼ teaspoon vanilla extract

Run warm water over can of peaches and remove peaches from can. Chop into pieces with large knife.

With steel knife in place, add peaches to work bowl with flavorings. Turn machine on and off several times, then let machine run until mixture is creamy. Serve immediately or refreeze.

SERVES 3 OR 4

FRUIT PARFAITS

1 cup oatmeal
½ cup dark brown sugar (half
   substitute, if desired)

5 tablespoons margarine, cut
   into pieces

Preheat oven to 350° F.

With steel knife in place, add all ingredients to work bowl. Turn machine on and off several times to mix well. Spread mixture in large baking pan and bake for 10 to 15 minutes, stirring occasionally. Let cool in pan.

FILLING

½ cup fresh fruit—strawberries,
   raspberries, blueberries,
   apricots, peaches: your
   choice
1 (8-ounce) container dry pot
   cheese
1 (8-ounce) container
   homogenized fruit-flavored
   yogurt

¼ cup confectioners' sugar
½ teaspoon vanilla
1 teaspoon fruit-flavored
   liqueur

With steel knife in place, chop fruit coarsely. Set aside, draining if needed.

Add pot cheese to work bowl. Turn machine on and off, then let run until smooth, scraping down sides if necessary. Add yogurt (using flavor congenial with fruit), sugar, vanilla, and liqueur (again using congenial flavor). Turn machine on and off to mix. Fold in fruit and chill well.

To serve, crumble some of the oatmeal mixture in the bottom of parfait glasses. Add some fruit mixture, more oatmeal mixture, and so on, ending with a few sprinkles of oatmeal mixture. Chill.

SERVES 6 TO 8

CHEESE DESSERT, ITALIAN STYLE

The partially skim milk ricotta cheese, slightly sweeter in flavor than cottage cheese, is excellent in this dessert. Ricotta does contain salt and is higher in fat content than the other cheeses recommended in this diet.

1 (16-ounce) container ricotta cheese, made from partially skim milk
2 tablespoons confectioners' sugar
2 tablespoons orange liqueur, or to taste
1½ tablespoons instant espresso coffee or same amount of regular instant coffee—NOT the freeze-dried variety
1 tablespoon unsweetened cocoa
Mint sprigs for garnish

With steel knife in place, add cheese and sugar to work bowl. Turn machine on and off several times. With machine running, add liqueur, then turn machine on and off to mix thoroughly.

Chill for several hours or overnight.

Mix coffee and cocoa together. Serve the cheese mixture in attractive dessert dishes, sprinkled with the coffee/cocoa mixture. Add a sprig of mint for color.

Variation: Other fruit-flavored liqueurs may be substituted for the orange.

SERVES 6 TO 8

MOCK DEVONSHIRE CREAM
(with strawberries or toast rounds)

The English country delicacy from Devonshire is a thick clotted cream made from nonhomogenized fresh farm milk. It is a treat to be eaten with scones and jam, fruit pies, or fruit. The following recipe, with added flavoring, will taste almost as good, particularly since it can be eaten safely on this diet.

Zest of ½ orange
⅓ cup sugar (use half regular and half substitute, if desired)
2 cups low-fat creamed cottage cheese

1 teaspoon vanilla
Skim milk (optional)
Whole strawberries (optional)
Melba rounds (optional)
Cinnamon sugar (optional)

With steel knife in place, add strips of orange zest and sugar to work bowl. Turn machine on and off, then let run until rind is reduced to a fine consistency. Add cottage cheese and vanilla. Turn machine on and off, then let run until completely smooth. Scrape down sides, if necessary. If mixture seems too thick (it should be of dipping consistency), add some skim milk, a teaspoon at a time, turning machine on and off until desired consistency is obtained. Chill thoroughly, at least 2 to 3 hours.

Serve mixture in small, attractive cups. Surround with whole strawberries. Or serve with crisp Melba rounds to dip or spread, and sprinkle with cinnamon sugar if desired.

Variation: This mixture is also delicious with chopped fresh or drained canned fruits folded into it.

SERVES 6 TO 8

EASIEST EVER PIECRUST

I cannot recommend many pies on this diet, but this easy and standard crust should be included to use with A Reasonable Strawberry Pie (recipe follows).

1 cup unsifted all-purpose flour
½ cup margarine (unsalted, if
*   desired), cut into pieces*

3 tablespoons ice water

With steel knife in place, add flour and margarine to work bowl. Turn machine on and off until mixture is consistency of cornmeal. With machine running, add ice water through feed tube and process only until ball of dough forms.

MAKES ENOUGH FOR AN 8- OR 9-INCH CRUST

A REASONABLE STRAWBERRY PIE

1 (8-inch) baked piecrust (see
*   index)*
1 quart fresh strawberries
½ cup sugar (or substitute)
1 tablespoon cornstarch

1 teaspoon lemon juice
Ricotta cheese (optional)
Low-fat creamed cottage
*   cheese, flavored if desired*
*   (optional)*

Arrange about half the berries in piecrust.
    With steel knife in place, add remaining berries to work bowl. Turn machine on and off until puréed.

In heavy saucepan, add puréed berries, sugar (or substitute), and cornstarch. Stir in lemon juice. Cook, stirring constantly, over medium heat until mixture thickens. Pour over berries in piecrust. Chill.

Serve with ricotta cheese or whipped low-fat creamed cottage cheese flavored with vanilla, almond, rum, Grand Marnier, or just plain.

SERVES 6 TO 8

Index